From Practitioner to Professor Designing Sustainable Cybersecurity Faculty Models

A Strategic Guide for Higher Education Leadership

by

Richard Lightcap, PhD

ISBN: 978-1-972154-01-4 (Paperback)
ISBN: 978-1-972154-00-7 (E-Book)

Library of Congress Control Number: 2026904488

Dedication

To Elizabeth, my unwavering companion and the steady light that has guided every step of this journey. In moments of uncertainty, you have offered clarity. In seasons of challenge, you have given strength. Your faith in me has been both anchor and horizon, grounding each effort while encouraging every aspiration.

This work bears your imprint in ways both visible and unseen. It was shaped by your patience when long hours demanded sacrifice and sustained by your encouragement when the pursuit of truth required perseverance. You have safeguarded the quiet spaces where ideas matured and hope endured.

May these pages reflect even a small measure of the grace, resilience, and love you extend so generously. This accomplishment is inseparable from your presence in my life. To you, who transforms ambition into purpose and effort into meaning.

Contents

Chapter 1: Why Cybersecurity Educator Recruitment Is Failing

1.1 Cybersecurity Faculty Shortages as an Institutional Risk

Cybersecurity programs now occupy a strategic position within higher education institutions. Universities depend on these programs to demonstrate workforce relevance, sustain employer confidence, attract enrollment, and justify continued investment in advanced technical infrastructure. When faculty recruitment falters, the effects cascade across curriculum quality, student experience, and institutional credibility. What initially appears as a manageable staffing inconvenience often evolves into a deeper structural risk. Over time, the inability to recruit consistently undermines the institution's capacity to deliver on its stated mission.

Institutions experiencing prolonged recruitment difficulty often underestimate the scope of the damage created by persistent vacancies. Faculty shortages limit the ability to revise curriculum in response to evolving threats, tools, and regulatory expectations. Program leaders divert attention from long term planning toward short-term coverage decisions and emergency scheduling. Strategic initiatives stall quietly as instructional continuity takes precedence. The program begins to operate reactively rather than intentionally.

As staffing pressure continues, instability becomes normalized through everyday decisions. Adjunct coverage expands beyond its original purpose as a supplemental resource. Full time faculty absorb additional sections without proportional reduction in advising, service, or administrative duties. Students encounter inconsistent instructional approaches across courses, even within the same sequence.

These patterns erode confidence gradually among learners, employers, and external reviewers.

The persistence of cybersecurity faculty shortages signals a systemic issue rather than an isolated hiring challenge. Institutions often acknowledge the symptoms while avoiding examination of root causes. Recruitment becomes treated as a recurring administrative task rather than a leadership responsibility requiring strategic design. This framing prevents learning from repeated failure and reinforces ineffective patterns. Without reframing the problem, institutions repeat the same searches with predictable outcomes.

1.2 The Limits of Market Based Explanations

Compensation disparity frequently dominates discussion of cybersecurity educator recruitment. Industry roles offer higher salaries, faster advancement, and broader mobility than academic positions. These realities influence professional decision making and shape early perceptions of teaching roles. However, compensation alone fails to explain the outcomes observed across institutions. Cybersecurity educators continue to enter academia despite full awareness of financial tradeoffs.

Consider the experience of a senior security engineer who spent years managing enterprise security operations and leading incident response teams. Over time, mentoring junior analysts and delivering internal training became the most fulfilling aspects of professional life. Teaching provided a sense of contribution missing from constant escalation cycles and crisis management. When an academic opportunity emerged, the engineer accepted reduced compensation intentionally. The decision reflected a shift in values rather than resignation.

This narrative reflects a broader pattern across educator experiences. Decisions to teach emerge from a complex value calculation involving purpose, autonomy, influence, and identity coherence. Financial considerations remain relevant but rarely function as the decisive factor alone. Institutions framing recruitment messaging almost exclusively around salary communicate a narrow understanding of candidate motivation. Candidates interpret this emphasis as misalignment rather than transparency.

When institutions fail to articulate non-monetary value clearly and credibly, compensation becomes the dominant visible variable. Under those conditions, industry predictably outcompetes academia. Recruitment improves only when institutions describe influence, instructional autonomy, intellectual engagement, and long-term impact as concrete features of the role. Without this clarity, even interested candidates disengage.

1.3 Cybersecurity as a Practice Formed Discipline

Cybersecurity developed primarily through operational necessity rather than academic lineage. The discipline matured within military, government, and enterprise environments where adversaries adapt continuously and consequences emerge quickly. Knowledge formation occurred through experience responding to breaches, audits, failures, and recovery efforts. Many foundational practices evolved long before cybersecurity achieved formal academic recognition. This history shapes how professionals interpret expertise and legitimacy.

A composite educator narrative illustrates this disciplinary trajectory. A former military cybersecurity officer transitioned into civilian infrastructure protection after years of managing sensitive systems under strict accountability. Teaching emerged gradually through mentoring responsibilities and internal training initiatives. Despite deep instructional capability, academic job postings emphasized credentials and research expectations misaligned with the officer's experience. The officer chose not to apply, interpreting the postings as exclusionary rather than aspirational.

Institutions applying legacy academic hiring norms to cybersecurity restrict their own access to qualified educators. Practitioners interpret job descriptions as signals of institutional rigidity. Search committees often confuse academic familiarity with instructional relevance. Recruitment fails not because candidates lack capability, but because institutions define qualification through inherited assumptions. Effective recruitment requires recalibration of standards without compromising academic integrity.

Recalibration demands intentional leadership involvement rather than automated screening. It requires recognition of cybersecurity as a discipline grounded in practice and judgment. Institutions unwilling to make this adjustment continue to experience shallow applicant pools. The problem persists until definitions of excellence align with disciplinary reality.

1.4 Professional Identity and the Decision to Teach

Cybersecurity professionals often possess strong occupational identities shaped by accountability and consequences. Their work involves protecting systems, advising leaders under uncertainty, and managing organizational risk. Decisions carry visible impact, reinforcing a sense of responsibility and professional seriousness. This identity influences how professionals evaluate potential career transitions. Teaching is assessed not as a job change, but as a transformation of role and influence.

Teaching cybersecurity requires identity transition rather than simple role substitution. The professional shifts from direct system protection toward indirect influence through student development. This transition demands internal validation and reflective judgment. Many professionals' question legitimacy and relevance during this period. Teaching becomes attractive only when it aligns with deeply held views of contribution and purpose.

One educator described extended hesitation rooted in concern over perceived distance from active threats. The educator feared losing professional credibility and relevance. Confidence emerged only after designing hands on learning experiences grounded in real incidents and operational decision making. Institutional environments supporting instructional autonomy accelerated this transition. Environments emphasizing rigid templates delayed it significantly.

Recruitment processes rarely acknowledge identity transition explicitly. Institutions often interpret hesitation as disinterest or indecision. Accelerated timelines and transactional messaging interrupt reflection rather than supporting it. Recruitment improves when leaders recognize teaching as an identity shift requiring respect, patience, and institutional support. Without this recognition, strong candidates disengage quietly.

1.5 Timing and Career Readiness in Cybersecurity Education

Career timing plays a decisive role in cybersecurity educator recruitment, yet institutions rarely account for it explicitly. Early career cybersecurity professionals focus on skill accumulation, certification attainment, and reputation building within demanding operational environments. Teaching during this stage often appears premature or risky. Many professionals fear insufficient authority or loss of momentum in a rapidly evolving field. As a result, early career candidates seldom pursue academic roles seriously.

Mid career professionals often experience a meaningful shift in perspective. Years of incident response, audit cycles, and organizational politics produce fatigue alongside accumulated confidence. Many professionals reach a point where mentoring junior colleagues provides greater satisfaction than constant escalation management. Teaching becomes a plausible next chapter rather than a departure from relevance. Institutions engaging candidates during this phase often encounter greater receptivity.

Later career professionals may seek stewardship and influence rather than direct operational control. Teaching offers a pathway to shape the field by developing future professionals. Some pursue flexible teaching arrangements while others seek full time academic appointments with leadership responsibility. Candidate readiness follows a gradual arc shaped by experience and reflection. Institutional hiring cycles rarely align with this arc, creating missed opportunities.

Recruitment fails when institutions rely on vacancy timing rather than candidate readiness. By the time a position opens, suitable candidates may remain unprepared for transition or already committed elsewhere. Strategic recruitment requires sustained relationship building rather than episodic searches. Institutions recognizing this reality develop pipelines rather than waiting for applications. Without this shift, recruitment outcomes remain inconsistent.

1.6 Role Design and the Signals Sent to Candidates

Role design communicates institutional priorities more clearly than recruitment language. Cybersecurity professionals evaluate role descriptions carefully and infer organizational health from structure and scope. Descriptions emphasizing broad coverage across unrelated domains signal overload and insufficient support. Candidates interpret such roles as unsustainable rather than challenging. Interest dissipates quickly when clarity proves absent.

One educator described declining an academic role after reviewing teaching expectations spanning multiple cybersecurity subfields without preparation support. The role description suggested accumulated unmet needs rather than intentional design. Despite enthusiasm for teaching, the educator concluded long term success would require constant triage. The decision reflected risk assessment rather than disinterest.

Strong candidates expect clarity regarding instructional domains, workload boundaries, curriculum authority, and professional development support. Ambiguity triggers concern rather than flexibility. When institutions fail to define roles precisely, candidates infer instability and limited institutional readiness. Recruitment succeeds when roles reflect respect for professional expertise and instructional quality.

Role design also influences long term retention. Educators who accept poorly defined roles often experience burnout quickly. Institutions then misinterpret attrition as individual failure rather than structural misalignment. Recruitment and retention remain inseparable in cybersecurity education. Sustainable recruitment begins with coherent role design.

1.7 Institutional Signals and Trust Formation During Recruitment

Cybersecurity professionals develop strong pattern recognition for organizational quality through years of risk evaluation. Recruitment processes generate signals rapidly and continuously. Delayed communication, conflicting messages, and vague expectations erode trust early. Candidates interpret silence as disorganization rather than deliberation.

An educator recounted withdrawing from a search after extended gaps between interviews. The absence of communication suggested unclear governance and weak coordination. In contrast, another institution communicated timelines clearly and introduced future colleagues early. The educator accepted the second offer despite lower compensation.

Trust forms through predictability, transparency, and respect for professional experience. Recruitment processes must align with expectations shaped by high accountability environments. Institutions signaling readiness and coherence attract candidates even under financial constraints. Those signaling uncertainty repel candidates regardless of salary.

Recruitment functions as a live demonstration of institutional culture. Candidates extrapolate from the hiring process to daily operations. Misalignment during recruitment predicts misalignment during employment. Leaders must treat recruitment interactions as consequential rather than procedural.

1.8 Screening Practices and the Limits of Traditional Proxies

Traditional academic screening practices rely heavily on proxies such as degrees, formal teaching experience, and research output. In cybersecurity educator recruitment, these proxies frequently misrepresent instructional potential. Many practitioners possess extensive informal teaching experience through mentoring, training programs, simulations, and security awareness initiatives. Conventional screening often fails to capture these contributions.

One educator entered academia after years leading enterprise training programs for security teams. Despite limited formal teaching experience, the educator demonstrated strong learning design capability and student engagement. Rigid screening criteria would have excluded this candidate entirely. Institutional flexibility enabled successful appointments.

Overreliance on research output creates additional misalignment. Some cybersecurity programs prioritize research, while many teachings focused programs emphasize curriculum relevance and applied learning. Applying identical expectations across contexts reduces fit and increases attrition. Recruitment improves when institutions align screening criteria with program mission.

Effective screening requires human judgment rather than automated filtering alone. Institutions must evaluate teaching readiness directly through evidence of mentoring, communication, and learning design. When screening practices align with instructional reality, candidate pools expand meaningfully. Without this alignment, recruitment remains artificially constrained.

1.9 The Cumulative Cost of Recruitment Failure

Recruitment failure in cybersecurity education produces effects extending far beyond unfilled positions. Existing faculty absorbs additional sections, increased advising loads, and expanded administrative responsibilities. Over time, this accumulation accelerates burnout and reduces instructional quality. Faculty energy shifts from innovation toward survival. Programs lose momentum even when enrollment demand remains strong.

Curriculum coherence suffers as staffing instability persists. Adjunct heavy coverage often produces uneven depth and inconsistent sequencing across courses. Faculty committees lack time and capacity to sustain shared standards. Students experience fragmentation and disengagement without understanding the cause. These outcomes damage program reputation gradually rather than abruptly.

Employers respond to inconsistency with reduced confidence. Internship pipelines weaken as preparation varies by section and instructor. Placement outcomes fluctuate unpredictably. Advisory boards raise concerns without clear remediation paths. Institutions then expend additional effort rebuilding trust once damage becomes visible.

Accreditation and assessment pressures intensify under staffing instability. Evidence collection becomes uneven. Learning outcomes coverage varies across terms. Program reviews require increased explanation rather than demonstration. Recruitment failure thus creates compliance risk alongside instructional risk. These cumulative costs rarely appear in hiring metrics, yet they determine long term viability.

1.10 Recruitment as Alignment Rather Than Acquisition

Recruitment succeeds when institutions pursue alignment rather than acquisition. Alignment occurs when professional identity, instructional need, career timing, and institutional culture converge. Acquisition treats hiring as procurement and focuses on filling roles quickly. Alignment treats hiring as a leadership function requiring design and intentionality.

Professional identity alignment requires recognition of cybersecurity as mission driven work. Candidates must see teaching as coherent with their sense of responsibility and contribution. Instructional alignment requires clarity around course domains and expectations. Career timing alignment acknowledges readiness for transition rather than immediate availability.

Institutional culture alignment influences trust and commitment. Educators thrive in environments supporting autonomy, accountability, and professional respect. Compensation supports alignment but never substitutes for it. Credentials establish baseline qualification but never ensure commitment. Recruitment improves when institutions design conditions supporting alignment deliberately.

This shift in perspective reframes recruitment outcomes. Institutions move from repeatedly filling vacancies toward building durable faculty communities. Retention improves because alignment sustains motivation. Recruitment becomes predictive rather than reactive. Leadership attention shifts from crisis management toward capacity building.

1.11 Why Lived Experience Evidence Matters

This book draws from lived experience because experience reveals how decisions unfold in practice. Quantitative labor data describes availability and demand. Lived experience explains willingness and hesitation. These perspectives complement each other rather than compete with each other.

Educator narratives illuminate how professionals interpret teaching roles. They reveal how purpose develops, how doubt emerges, and how institutional signals influence interpretation. These narratives expose decision logic invisible to surface level analysis. Leaders gain insight into candidate reasoning rather than relying on assumption.

Lived experience also surfaces patterns across diverse contexts. While individual stories differ, themes recur consistently. These patterns enable translation from narrative into strategy. Recruitment grounded in experience produces practical insight for design and leadership.

Without lived experience, recruitment strategies remain speculative. With it, leaders gain evidence rooted in real decision making. This approach strengthens credibility and precision. Institutions adopting experience informed recruitment reduce misalignment systematically.

1.12 Transition From Diagnosis to Design

This chapter establishes diagnosis through sustained examination of recruitment failure. Cybersecurity educator recruitment fails for identifiable reasons rooted in misalignment rather than scarcity. Institutions misinterpret professional identity, underestimate timing effects, misdesign roles, and send unintended signals. These failures are repeated because underlying assumptions remain unchallenged.

Diagnosis alone does not resolve the problem. Institutions require concrete frameworks translating insight into practice. Leaders need tools enabling better role design, screening, and engagement. Recruitment must move beyond habit toward intentional architecture.

The next chapter begins this transition by defining the cybersecurity educator institutions actually need. This definition moves beyond credentials toward capability, motivation, and readiness. It establishes a profile supporting practical hiring decisions. Design replaces diagnosis as the organizing principle.

1.13 Leadership Responsibility Across Recruitment Functions

Cybersecurity educator recruitment rarely succeeds through isolated effort. Human resources, academic leadership, and faculty governance all influence outcomes. When responsibility fragments, misalignment grows. Each group assumes another group owns the problem. Recruitment stalls while accountability diffuses.

Human resources teams often manage process efficiency, compliance, and policy alignment. These functions matter, yet they cannot define instructional needs or professional fit alone. Without close collaboration with academic leadership, HR screening criteria misrepresent capability. Candidates encounter confusing or contradictory signals early in the process. Trust erodes before substantive conversation begins.

Academic leaders shape role design, curriculum scope, and instructional expectations. When leaders fail to articulate needs clearly, recruitment inherits ambiguity. Search committees default to familiar proxies rather than intentional evaluation. Candidates sense uncertainty and disengage. Recruitment failure reflects leadership silence rather than market scarcity.

Shared responsibility requires explicit coordination. Leaders must align role design, screening logic, messaging, and onboarding support. Recruitment improves when leadership treats hiring as a strategic system rather than a procedural sequence. Without this integration, improvement remains elusive.

1.14 The Educator Value Proposition Institutions Rarely Articulate

Higher education cannot compete directly with industry compensation models. Institutions succeed by articulating a coherent value proposition grounded in meaning, autonomy, and influence. Many institutions assume this value proposition speaks for itself. Candidates rarely share this assumption.

Cybersecurity educators often seek visible impact. Teaching offers the opportunity to shape future professionals and influence workforce quality. Institutions frequently reference impact abstractly without operational clarity. Candidates want evidence of real influence through curriculum control, pedagogical freedom, and program development opportunities.

Autonomy functions as another critical value dimension. Cybersecurity professionals operate in environments requiring judgment and discretion. Teaching environments restricting instructional decision making undermines perceived value. Institutions supporting faculty agency attract candidates even under financial constraint.

Intellectual engagement and stability also matter. Educators seek environments encouraging continuous learning without constant crisis escalation. Teaching offers space for reflection and growth when supported properly. Institutions articulating these conditions clearly improve recruitment yield. Without clarity, candidates remain skeptical.

1.15 Recruitment Messaging and Candidate Interpretation

Recruitment messaging serves as an early signal of institutional culture. Generic language produces generic outcomes. Cybersecurity professionals read postings carefully and interpret omissions as intentionally as inclusions. Messaging lacking specificity suggests limited understanding of the field.

Candidates evaluate whether institutions respect cybersecurity as a discipline requiring depth and currency. Vague references to teaching technology courses undermine credibility. Clear articulation of instructional domains builds confidence. Messaging should reflect familiarity with professional practice rather than borrowed templates.

Narrative clarity matters as much as technical detail. Candidates respond to language conveying mission and seriousness. Messaging framing teaching as content delivery labor discourages engagement. Messaging framing teaching as professional contribution invites reflection.

Recruitment improves when messaging aligns with lived professional experience. Institutions demonstrating awareness of cybersecurity realities signal readiness. Those relying on generic academic language appear disconnected. Messaging functions as both invitation and filter.

1.16 Reframing Recruitment as Institutional Design

Recruitment outcomes reflect institutional design choices rather than chance. Role clarity, screening logic, communication practices, and onboarding support shape candidate interpretation. Institutions often attempt improvement through incremental process adjustments. Without addressing design fundamentals, these efforts fail.

Viewing recruitment as design reframes leadership responsibility. Leaders must evaluate whether structures support professional transition into teaching. This evaluation includes curriculum governance, workload balance, mentoring, and resource availability. Design determines whether recruitment efforts convert interest into commitment.

Institutions redesigning recruitment intentionally observe predictable improvement. Applicant pools deepen. Offer acceptance increases. Early attrition declines. Faculty engagement strengthens. These outcomes arise from alignment rather than persuasion.

Reframing recruitment as institutional design sets the foundation for sustainable growth. It shifts focus from filling vacancies toward building capacity. Leadership moves from reactive problem solving toward proactive stewardship. Recruitment becomes a lever for program strength rather than a recurring crisis.

1.17 Why This Book Centers Educator Lived Experience

Many professional guides rely on abstract models or generalized workforce data. While useful for trend analysis, such approaches rarely explain how individuals experience career decisions in practice. Cybersecurity educator recruitment requires understanding internal reasoning, not just external conditions. Lived experience evidence provides access to motivation, hesitation, and interpretation unavailable through quantitative measures alone. This perspective reveals why similarly qualified candidates make different decisions when encountering the same opportunity.

Educator narratives illuminate how identity, purpose, and timing interact during career transitions. They show how professionals weigh legitimacy, influence, and perceived impact. These narratives also expose how institutional signals shape meaning rather than simply conveying information. Leaders gain insight into candidate reasoning rather than relying on assumption or stereotype. Recruitment design improves when informed by interpretation rather than inference.

Experience based evidence also reveals consistency across diverse contexts. Individual stories vary, yet patterns recur. These patterns allow translation from narrative into strategy without reducing individuals to caricatures. Institutions applying such insight gain precision without sacrificing empathy. Recruitment becomes informed rather than speculative.

This book draws deliberately from educator experience to ground strategy in reality. It does not reject quantitative data, but it refuses to treat data as sufficient alone. Experience complements metrics by explaining why numbers move. Leaders equipped with this perspective design recruitment systems capable of sustained success.

1.18 What Changes When Institutions Apply Evidence Informed Recruitment

Institutions applying evidence informed recruitment observe predictable changes. Applicant pools expand in quality and diversity. Candidate engagement deepens earlier in the process. Offer acceptance rates improve even when compensation remains constrained. These outcomes result from alignment rather than persuasion.

Recruitment processes become more deliberate and less reactive. Leaders invest time in role design before posting positions. Screening criteria reflect instructional capability rather than inherited proxies. Communication becomes clearer and more predictable. Candidates respond positively to professionalism and coherence.

Retention also improves as alignment strengthens. Faculty enter roles with realistic expectations and institutional support. Early burnout declines as role design reflects sustainability. Program stability increases, allowing curriculum maturation and student engagement. Recruitment and retention reinforce each other rather than competing for attention.

Evidence informed recruitment shifts leadership posture. Institutions move from explaining failure toward designing success. Hiring becomes a strategic capability rather than a recurring challenge. Over time, faculty communities strengthen rather than churn.

1.19 Summary of the Recruitment Failure Diagnosis

Cybersecurity educator recruitment fails for recurring and identifiable reasons. Institutions treat recruitment as procurement rather than alignment. Role design often signals overload and limited influence. Screening criteria exclude practitioner pathways unintentionally. Hiring timelines misalign with candidate readiness. Institutional signals erode trust among risk aware professionals.

These failures persist because they feel familiar. Leaders rely on inherited academic models without recalibration. Each unsuccessful search reinforces assumptions rather than challenging them. Recruitment becomes ritual rather than reflection. Programs absorb the consequences quietly.

This chapter demonstrates recruitment failure reflects design choices rather than labor scarcity. When institutions change assumptions, outcomes change. Recruitment improves through intentional alignment rather than increased effort alone. The problem becomes solvable once defined correctly.

Diagnosis provides clarity but not completion. Institutions require frameworks translating insight into action. Without such translation, understanding remains academic rather than operational. The next chapter begins this translation.

1.20 Transition Toward the Ideal Cybersecurity Educator Profile

Recruitment redesign begins with clarity regarding who the institution truly needs. Many searches fail because leaders cannot articulate desired educator attributes beyond credentials. Degrees and certifications function as proxies rather than definitions. Effective recruitment requires a richer understanding of capability, motivation, and readiness.

The next chapter develops a research driven profile of the cybersecurity educator suited for contemporary higher education. This profile emphasizes instructional capability, professional credibility, and alignment with institutional mission. It moves beyond titles toward practical indicators leaders can evaluate during hiring. The profile provides a foundation for interview design, screening refinement, and onboarding support.

This transition marks a shift from diagnosis to design. The focus moves from understanding failure toward constructing success. Recruitment becomes intentional rather than habitual. Chapter 2 establishes the core framework supporting this transformation.

Chapter 2: How Cybersecurity Professionals Decide to Become Educators

2.1 Teaching as a Deliberate Career Decision

Cybersecurity professionals rarely arrive in teaching roles by accident. The decision to become an educator emerges through extended reflection rather than spontaneous opportunity. Professionals evaluate teaching alongside identity, credibility, and long term contribution. This evaluation unfolds gradually as experience accumulates and professional perspective deepens. Teaching represents a directional shift rather than a lateral move.

Many professionals initially dismiss teaching as incompatible with serious cybersecurity work. Early assumptions frame academia as detached from operational reality. These assumptions persist until counter experiences emerge, often through mentoring or training responsibilities. Once professionals experience instructional impact directly, teaching begins to reenter consideration. The decision space expands slowly rather than abruptly.

Teaching appeals when professionals perceive it as a continuation of service rather than a retreat from relevance. Cybersecurity educators often describe teaching as protecting systems indirectly through people. This reframing transforms teaching from abstraction into mission aligned work. Institutions recognizing this framing engage candidates more effectively. Those ignoring it encounter resistance.

Recruitment improves when leaders understand teaching decisions unfold over time. Treating teaching as a reactive option misrepresents professional reasoning. Institutions must respect the deliberative nature of the decision. Without this respect, recruitment efforts misfire regardless of effort.

2.2 The Role of Meaning and Purpose in Career Transition

Meaning plays a central role in the transition from practitioner to educator. Cybersecurity work often carries high intensity and constant escalation. Over time, professionals reassess what sustained contribution looks like. Purpose shifts from immediate threat response toward longer term impact. Teaching emerges as a vehicle for meaning preservation rather than loss.

Educators frequently describe moments of dissonance preceding the transition. Despite technical success, daily work begins to feel repetitive or narrowly reactive. Mentoring junior colleagues provides renewed engagement. Instruction allows professionals to step back from constant urgency while remaining connected to mission. This recalibration reshapes career priorities.

Institutions recruiting educators must recognize meaning as a legitimate decision driver. Candidates seek roles aligning professional values with institutional purpose. Generic recruitment language rarely addresses this dimension. Messaging emphasizing coverage or compliance fails to engage purpose driven reasoning.

Recruitment improves when institutions articulate how teaching contributes to societal resilience. Educators respond to narratives connecting classroom impact to workforce preparedness. Purpose oriented messaging signals seriousness rather than sentiment. Without this framing, institutions struggle to convert interest into commitment.

2.3 Confidence, Credibility, and Readiness to Teach

Confidence influences readiness to teach as strongly as competence. Cybersecurity professionals often hesitate despite deep expertise. Many question whether experience translates effectively into instruction. Concerns center on legitimacy, relevance, and authority within an academic environment. These concerns delay transition even when interest exists.

Educators often report a threshold moment where confidence crystallizes. This moment may follow successful mentoring, training delivery, or curriculum design. Once professionals witness learning outcomes directly, self-doubt recedes. Teaching shifts from aspiration toward attainable role. Institutions supporting early instructional experimentation accelerate this transition.

Credential requirements influence confidence indirectly. Rigid emphasis on degrees may reinforce doubt among capable practitioners. Flexible pathways validating experience reduce psychological barriers. Confidence grows when institutions signal respect for operational expertise. Recruitment succeeds when readiness receives support rather than skepticism.

Leaders must distinguish capability from readiness. Capability exists long before readiness emerges. Recruitment strategies recognizing this gap engage candidates earlier. Without this distinction, institutions wait too long and lose candidates elsewhere.

2.4 Mentorship and Exposure as Catalysts for Teaching Identity

Mentorship functions as a powerful catalyst in educator identity formation. Many cybersecurity educators trace teaching interest to influential mentors. Exposure to effective educators reshapes perception of academia. Mentorship normalizes the transition rather than romanticizing it. These relationships legitimize teaching as serious professional work.

Exposure often occurs informally. Guest lectures, internal training, conference workshops, and collaborative curriculum projects introduce professionals to instructional roles. These experiences reduce uncertainty through practice. Teaching becomes familiar rather than abstract. Institutions fostering exposure create pipelines organically.

One educator described shadowing a faculty member during a semester long course. Observing classroom dynamics and curriculum design demystified teaching. Confidence followed familiarity. Without this exposure, teaching would have remained theoretical.

Recruitment improves when institutions invest in exposure pathways. Mentorship programs, practitioner fellowships, and adjunct onboarding create low risk entry points. These structures support identity formation rather than forcing decisions prematurely. Without exposure, readiness rarely emerges.

2.5 Early Career Signals and the Formation of Teaching Interest

Interest in teaching rarely appears suddenly within cybersecurity careers. Instead, it develops through early signals encountered long before formal transition becomes plausible. These signals often emerge during the first years of professional practice through informal mentoring, peer guidance, or internal knowledge sharing. Professionals who find satisfaction in explaining complex concepts or supporting others begin to recognize an instructional inclination. This recognition may remain dormant while career demands remain intense.

Many educators describe early moments when teaching instincts surfaced unexpectedly. A professional asked to onboard a new analyst discovers enjoyment in translating abstract risk into practical understanding. Another finds fulfillment leading tabletop exercises or security awareness sessions. These moments generate quiet satisfaction without immediate career implications. Teaching interest forms as a latent trait rather than an explicit goal.

Institutions rarely notice these early signals. Recruitment strategies often target candidates already seeking academic roles. By the time a professional self identifies as an educator, institutions have missed years of opportunity for engagement. Early recognition enables earlier cultivation.

Strategic recruitment benefits from understanding early interest formation. Institutions investing in practitioner engagement activities build awareness and familiarity. Teaching interest grows through exposure rather than persuasion. Without early signals, later recruitment faces unnecessary resistance.

2.6 Professional Fatigue and the Search for Sustainable Contribution

Professional fatigue functions as a common inflection point in cybersecurity educator decisions. Continuous exposure to escalation cycles, regulatory pressure, and incident response produces cumulative strain. Even successful professionals experience diminished satisfaction over time. Fatigue triggers reassessment of long-term sustainability rather than immediate exit.

Many educators describe fatigue not as burnout but as saturation. The work remains important, yet its repetitive urgency erodes engagement. Mentoring and teaching activities offer relief by shifting focus from crisis response toward development. Instruction provides rhythm and reflection absent from operational environments.

Teaching becomes attractive as a form of sustainable contribution. Professionals perceive education as impactful without constant escalation. This perception reframes teaching from retreat to strategic redirection. Institutions recognizing this motivation engage candidates more effectively.

Recruitment messaging rarely addresses sustainability directly. Candidates infer institutional values through silence. Explicit recognition of professional fatigue signals empathy rather than weakness. Institutions acknowledging sustainability concerns foster trust and openness.

2.7 Perceived Legitimacy and the Role of Institutional Validation

Perceived legitimacy shapes readiness to teach as strongly as interest or competence. Cybersecurity professionals often question whether academic environments value operational experience. Concerns center on credibility among peers and authority in the classroom. Without validation, hesitation persists.

Institutional signals play a decisive role in legitimacy formation. Hiring criteria emphasizing degrees alone reinforce doubt among practitioners. Institutions recognizing experiential knowledge reduce psychological barriers. Validation emerges when leaders acknowledge professional expertise explicitly.

One educator described relief upon hearing a dean frame operational experience as essential to curriculum relevance. This validation shifted self-perception from outsider to contributor. Teaching confidence followed institutional recognition. Without validation, interest might have faded.

Recruitment improves when institutions design validation intentionally. Language, policy, and leadership behavior communicate legitimacy. Validation accelerates readiness and commitment. Without it, capable educators remain on the margins.

2.8 Teaching as Identity Integration Rather Than Replacement

Cybersecurity professionals rarely abandon practitioner identity when entering teaching. Instead, teaching integrates identity rather than replacing it. Educators continue to view themselves as security professionals who teach rather than teachers who once practiced. This distinction matters deeply.

Identity integration allows educators to maintain credibility and relevance. Teaching becomes an extension of professional service. Students benefit from instructors who embody the field rather than observe it from distance. Institutions supporting identity integration strengthen instructional quality.

Some educators maintain industry engagement alongside teaching. Consulting, research collaboration, or advisory roles sustain relevance. Institutions restricting external engagement undermine identity integration. Flexibility supports retention.

Recruitment succeeds when teaching roles allow identity continuity. Institutions framing teaching as departure from practice discourage candidates. Those framing teaching as professional evolution attract commitment. Identity integration anchors long term success.

2.9 Risk Perception and Decision Framing in Career Transition

Cybersecurity professionals evaluate career transitions through a risk oriented lens shaped by years of threat modeling and consequence management. Decisions rarely hinge on optimism alone. Professionals assess downside exposure, uncertainty, and reversibility before committing. Teaching decisions follow this same evaluative pattern rather than emotional impulse. Institutions often underestimate the analytical rigor applied to career change.

Perceived risks include loss of professional relevance, reduced credibility, and limited mobility. Professionals worry about reentry into industry should teaching prove unsatisfying. These concerns intensify when institutions lack clear pathways for professional engagement. Recruitment efforts ignoring risk perception fail to address a core decision driver.

Educators who transition successfully often describe reframing risk through exposure and validation. Short term teaching experiences reduce uncertainty. Institutional support reduces perceived irreversibility. Recruitment improves when leaders acknowledge risk explicitly rather than minimizing it.

Risk framing influences pacing as well as outcome. Professionals move toward teaching incrementally. Institutions demanding immediate commitment disrupt decision logic. Respect for risk perception increases trust and engagement.

2.10 Social Influence and the Weight of Peer Perception

Peer perception shapes teaching decisions more than institutions often realize. Cybersecurity professionals operate within communities where credibility and reputation matter deeply. Career transitions receive scrutiny, both explicit and implicit. Teaching decisions unfold within this social context.

Some professionals fear peer interpretation of teaching as disengagement from serious work. Others worry about diminished status within technical communities. These perceptions persist even when inaccurate. Educators describe internal negotiation between personal fulfillment and perceived external judgment.

Positive peer models counteract hesitation. Seeing respected professionals teach legitimizes the path. Peer affirmation reduces doubt and normalizes transition. Institutions benefiting from visible educator role models gain recruitment advantage.

Recruitment strategies rarely leverage peer influence intentionally. Institutions could amplify educator voices and trajectories. Visibility shifts perception from anomaly to option. Peer context shapes decision readiness profoundly.

2.11 Institutional Readiness as a Determinant of Commitment

Teaching decisions depend not only on individual readiness but also on institutional readiness. Professionals evaluate whether institutions can support instructional success. This evaluation includes resources, governance, and leadership coherence. Commitment follows confidence in institutional capability.

Educators describe assessing classroom infrastructure, lab support, and curriculum flexibility during recruitment. Weak signals undermine enthusiasm quickly. Strong signals build confidence and accelerate commitment. Institutional readiness functions as a form of risk mitigation.

Leadership transparency matters during this assessment. Honest discussion of constraints builds trust. Overpromising damages credibility. Educators prefer clarity over aspiration.

Recruitment improves when institutions demonstrate preparedness rather than ambition alone. Readiness communicates respect for educator professionalism. Commitment follows environments designed for success.

2.12 Synthesis of the Educator Decision Model

Cybersecurity educator decisions emerge through an interaction of identity, timing, risk perception, social context, and institutional readiness. No single factor determines outcome. Decisions unfold gradually through evaluation and exposure. Recruitment succeeds when institutions align with this process.

Teaching becomes viable when professionals integrate identity rather than replace it. Timing aligns when experience supports reflection. Risk reduces through validation and reversibility. Social influence legitimizes transition. Institutional readiness anchors commitment.

This model explains variation across individuals and institutions. Some professionals transition smoothly while others disengage. Outcomes reflect alignment rather than motivation alone. Recruitment strategies succeed when designed around this model.

The next chapter operationalizes this synthesis. It translates decision logic into practical hiring frameworks. Leaders gain tools to recognize readiness and support transition. Design replaces assumption as the organizing principle.

Chapter 3: Early Influences and the Formation of Cybersecurity Educator Identity

3.1 Early Exposure to Teaching as a Latent Influence

Early exposure to teaching often shapes cybersecurity educator identity long before formal career transitions occur. These exposures rarely appear as decisive moments at the time. Instead, they function as latent influences that surface later during professional reflection. Individuals recall early experiences of explanation, guidance, or demonstration as formative only in hindsight. Teaching interest develops quietly beneath the demands of technical work.

Many cybersecurity educators describe early opportunities to assist peers during academic or training environments. Helping classmates understand networking concepts or security fundamentals produced unexpected satisfaction. These moments rarely triggered immediate career reconsideration. They planted a sense of instructional capability that remained dormant. Over time, these experiences accumulated psychological weight.

Institutions rarely recognize early exposure as a recruitment signal. Traditional hiring focuses on immediate availability rather than formative experience. Early teaching exposure often goes undocumented and unacknowledged. Recruitment strategies ignoring this dimension miss foundational identity formation.

Understanding early exposure allows institutions to design earlier engagement pathways. Recognition of latent teaching influence reframes candidate development. Teaching identity begins earlier than institutions assume. Recruitment improves when early exposure receives attention rather than dismissal.

3.2 Academic Experiences and Perceptions of Instructional Quality

Academic experiences play a critical role in shaping perceptions of teaching credibility. Cybersecurity professionals often recall instructors who either inspired confidence or reinforced skepticism toward academia. Instructional quality influences long term attitudes toward teaching roles. Positive academic experiences legitimize teaching as serious professional work.

Educators frequently describe formative instructors who blended theory with applied relevance. These instructors demonstrated mastery without detachment. Exposure to such models reframed perceptions of academia. Teaching appeared compatible with professional rigor. Interest followed legitimacy.

Negative academic experiences also shape identity. Some professionals encountered outdated curricula or disengaged instructors. These experiences fostered skepticism toward teaching environments. Professionals questioned whether academia valued relevance. Teaching interest diminished accordingly.

Institutions influence future educator pipelines through instructional quality. Every classroom interaction shapes perception. Faculty behavior influences not only students but future educators. Recruitment success depends partly on present instructional credibility.

3.3 Mentorship as a Structuring Forcc in Educator Identity

Mentorship consistently emerges as a structuring influence in cybersecurity educator identity formation. Many educators attribute teaching interest to mentors who recognized instructional aptitude. Mentors normalize teaching as a viable professional pathway. This normalization reduces psychological barriers. Identity shifts accelerate through trusted validation.

Mentorship often occurs informally rather than through structured programs. Senior professionals invite juniors to assist with training or documentation. These opportunities foster instructional confidence. Teaching becomes familiar rather than abstract. Identity develops through practice.

Educators frequently describe mentors who reframed teaching as service rather than retreat. This reframing counters industry narratives equating relevance with constant escalation. Mentors provide permission to value education. Without mentorship, teaching interest may remain suppressed.

Institutions benefit when mentorship pathways receive institutional support. Structured mentoring programs amplify organic influence. Recruitment improves when mentorship connects professionals to teaching environments. Identity formation thrives under guidance.

3.4 Early Professional Teaching Moments and Confidence Formation

Early professional teaching moments function as confidence catalysts. Cybersecurity professionals often encounter situations requiring explanation to non-specialists. Leading training sessions, onboarding new hires, or conducting awareness briefings reveal instructional ability. Confidence emerges through successful communication rather than credentials.

Educators frequently describe surprise at instructional effectiveness. Translating complex concepts into accessible language produced positive feedback. These moments challenged self-perceptions. Teaching shifted from hypothetical interest to demonstrated capability. Confidence expanded incrementally.

Institutions rarely capture these early teaching moments during recruitment. Screening processes overlook informal instructional experience. Professionals struggle to articulate teaching capability without prompting. Recruitment criteria ignoring these experiences exclude capable educators.

Recognizing early teaching moments improves candidate evaluation. Institutions can surface instructional evidence through narrative inquiry. Confidence grows when experience receives validation. Recruitment benefits from attention to formative teaching practice.

3.5 The Influence of Industry Training and Knowledge Transfer Roles

Industry training roles exert a powerful influence on the development of cybersecurity educator identity. Many professionals encounter teaching through responsibilities unrelated to formal instruction. Leading internal training sessions, developing onboarding materials, and facilitating security awareness programs introduce instructional practice organically. These experiences normalize teaching as part of professional contribution rather than as a separate vocation. Identity formation occurs through repetition rather than declaration.

Educators frequently describe industry training responsibilities as confidence building experiences. Explaining security concepts to diverse audiences requires clarity, patience, and adaptability. Positive learner feedback reinforces instructional aptitude. Teaching competence emerges through demonstrated effectiveness rather than credential acquisition. Over time, professionals begin to view instruction as a strength rather than an obligation.

Institutions often undervalue industry training experience during recruitment. Job postings emphasize classroom teaching history while ignoring internal instructional roles. Candidates struggle to translate industry training into academic language. Recruitment processes rarely invite narrative explanation of instructional practice. This oversight excludes capable educators unintentionally.

Recognizing industry training experience broadens recruitment pools meaningfully. Institutions benefit from educators experienced in translating complex content for varied audiences. Instructional effectiveness transfers across contexts. Recruitment improves when leaders evaluate teaching capability holistically rather than formally.

3.6 Exposure to Students and the Emotional Dimension of Teaching

Direct exposure to students plays a critical role in solidifying teaching identity. Professionals often describe moments when learner engagement produced emotional resonance. Observing understanding develop through explanation generates fulfillment distinct from operational success. Teaching satisfaction derives from relational impact rather than technical resolution. These experiences anchor long term interest.

Educators recount guest lectures or adjunct roles as transformative experiences. Interaction with motivated learners reframes professional purpose. Classroom dialogue reveals influence extending beyond immediate task completion. Teaching begins to feel consequential in new ways. Emotional connection strengthens commitment.

Institutions influence exposure frequency through access design. Guest lecturing opportunities and practitioner partnerships create early student interaction. Without these opportunities, professionals remain disconnected from teaching environments. Recruitment relies on exposure rather than persuasion.

Teaching identity stabilizes through repeated student interaction. Emotional engagement reinforces instructional motivation. Institutions fostering exposure cultivate future educators organically. Recruitment becomes a byproduct of engagement rather than solicitation.

3.7 Family, Community, and Cultural Influences on Teaching Orientation

Family and community context shape attitudes toward teaching more than institutions often acknowledge. Many educators describe early exposure to teaching through family members working in education. These environments normalize instructional service as meaningful work. Teaching becomes culturally legitimate rather than peripheral. Identity formation absorbs these values gradually.

Community involvement also influences orientation toward education. Professionals engaged in volunteer teaching, coaching, or mentoring encounter instructional satisfaction outside formal roles. These experiences reinforce teaching as social contribution. Community recognition strengthens instructional identity. Teaching interest develops across life domains.

Educators often reflect on cultural narratives equating teaching with service. These narratives counter industry emphasis on financial success alone. Teaching aligns with broader life values. Recruitment benefits when institutions recognize cultural context.

Ignoring family and community influence limits understanding of motivation. Recruitment strategies focusing solely on professional trajectory miss critical drivers. Teaching identity forms holistically rather than professionally alone. Institutions acknowledging this complexity recruit more effectively.

3.8 Early Discouragement and the Suppression of Teaching Identity

Early discouragement plays a significant role in suppressing teaching interest. Some professionals encounter negative messages regarding academia during early career stages. Peers may frame teaching as disengagement from serious work. These narratives discourage exploration even when interest exists. Identity formation stalls under social pressure.

Educators describe internal conflict between curiosity and caution. Interest in teaching competes with fear of diminished credibility. Discouragement does not eliminate interest entirely. It delays expression and exploration. Teaching identity becomes latent rather than absent.

Institutional barriers amplify discouragement. Rigid credential requirements and dismissive language reinforce doubt. Professionals interpret these signals as rejection. Recruitment loses candidates long before formal application. Suppression operates silently.

Institutions counter discouragement through inclusive messaging and validation. Visible educator pathways normalize transition. Supportive signals revive suppressed interest. Recruitment improves when institutions address discouragement intentionally.

3.9 Validation Through Early Teaching Success

Early teaching success plays a decisive role in solidifying cybersecurity educator identity. Professionals often describe moments when instructional efforts produced visible learner progress. These moments provide validation distinct from technical achievement. Teaching success reframes self perception from capable practitioner to effective educator. Confidence grows through demonstrated impact rather than formal recognition.

Educators recount early sessions where complex security concepts became accessible to learners. Positive feedback from students or trainees reinforces instructional legitimacy.

These experiences counter lingering doubt regarding teaching ability. Teaching shifts from aspirational interest to proven competence. Identity integration accelerates as confidence stabilizes.

Institutions influence access to early teaching success through opportunity design. Guest lectures, workshops, and supervised adjunct roles create safe environments for experimentation. Without structured access, professionals lack feedback loops. Recruitment improves when institutions facilitate early instructional validation.

Teaching success also shapes long term commitment. Educators experiencing early affirmation pursue teaching more deliberately. Those lacking validation remain uncertain. Recruitment strategies should prioritize opportunities for early success rather than waiting for full commitment.

3.10 Narrative Identity and the Retelling of Professional Experience

Cybersecurity educator identity forms through narrative interpretation of experience. Professionals construct meaning by retelling career stories through an instructional lens. Past incidents, failures, and recoveries gain new purpose as teaching material. Teaching allows professionals to reinterpret experience as transferable wisdom. Identity evolves through storytelling.

Educators describe reframing career milestones as lessons rather than achievements. Breach response becomes case study material. Compliance challenges become instructional examples. This narrative shift transforms memory into pedagogy. Teaching identity deepens through reinterpretation.

Institutions supporting narrative integration strengthen educator confidence. Curriculum design allowing experiential storytelling validates professional history. Rigid content templates restrict narrative expression. Educators thrive when permitted to teach through lived experience.

Recruitment improves when institutions invite narrative sharing during hiring. Candidates articulate identity through story. Leaders assess alignment through interpretation. Narrative clarity predicts instructional effectiveness.

3.11 Accumulation of Influence and the Desire to Shape the Field

Desire to shape the field motivates many cybersecurity educators. Over time, professionals seek influence beyond immediate organizational boundaries. Teaching offers leverage through multiplicative impact. Educators influence not one system, but many through students. This accumulation of influence aligns with professional maturation.

Educators describe frustration with recurring organizational failures. Teaching provides opportunity to address root causes through education. Instruction becomes a form of preventive control. Identity shifts toward stewardship rather than reaction. Teaching aligns with long term vision.

Institutions attracting such educators emphasize influence explicitly. Program development, curriculum leadership, and industry engagement opportunities appeal strongly. Roles limited to delivery discourage commitment. Recruitment succeeds when influence appears genuine.

Influence oriented motivation sustains long term engagement. Educators remain committed when impact feels visible. Recruitment benefits from recognizing this driver. Teaching becomes purposeful rather than procedural.

3.12 Synthesis of Early Influences in Educator Identity Formation

Early influences shape cybersecurity educator identity through cumulative effect rather than singular events. Exposure to teaching, mentorship, validation, and narrative reinterpretation interact over time. Identity forms gradually through reflection and experience. Teaching emerges as integrated professional expression rather than departure.

Discouragement and validation coexist within identity formation. Suppression delays but rarely eliminates interest. Supportive environments revive latent identity. Institutions play a decisive role through signaling and opportunity design.

This chapter demonstrates identity formation begins long before recruitment. Institutions engaging early influence gain advantage. Recruitment strategies succeed when aligned with identity development rather than end stage selection. Early engagement produces durable commitment.

The next chapter shifts focus from identity formation to institutional interaction. It examines how organizational structures, policies, and cultures influence educator decisions. Recruitment outcomes depend on institutional readiness as much as individual motivation.

Chapter 4: Institutional Structures and the Decision Environment for Cybersecurity Educator Recruitment

4.1 Institutions as Decision Environments Rather Than Neutral Platforms

Higher education institutions often view themselves as neutral platforms where talent enters through formal processes. This assumption obscures the reality experienced by cybersecurity professionals. Institutions function as decision environments shaping interpretation, confidence, and willingness to commit. Policies, structures, and norms influence candidate reasoning before interviews begin. Recruitment outcomes reflect environmental design rather than applicant quality alone.

Cybersecurity professionals assess institutions through accumulated signals. Governance structures, approval cycles, and role clarity communicate readiness or fragility. Candidates infer institutional competence from how decisions occur rather than from mission statements. These inferences shape trust early in the process. Recruitment fails when institutions underestimate this evaluative behavior.

Decision environments influence perceived risk. Ambiguity increases uncertainty and discourages commitment. Clarity reduces cognitive load and supports deliberate choice. Institutions ignoring environmental influence misattribute failure to candidate shortage. Effective recruitment begins with environmental self-assessment.

Institutions redesigning decision environments observe improved engagement. Candidates remain active longer. Conversations deepen rather than stall. Recruitment improves without increased advertising. Environment matters more than volume.

4.2 Policy Density and Its Impact on Candidate Interpretation

Policy density shapes how cybersecurity professionals interpret institutional seriousness. Extensive policies may signal rigor or rigidity depending on presentation and application. Candidates accustomed to regulated environments evaluate policy through functionality rather than quantity. Policies detached from practice raise concern. Recruitment suffers when policy overwhelms purpose.

Cybersecurity professionals operate within frameworks balancing control and adaptability. Policies supporting judgment enhance confidence. Policies constraining discretion erode trust. During recruitment, candidates assess whether policy enables or restricts professional contribution. Interpretation occurs rapidly.

One educator described withdrawing after encountering layers of approval required for minor curriculum updates. The process suggested misalignment with cybersecurity realities. Teaching appeared constrained rather than empowered. Interest diminished accordingly.

Institutions benefit from policy transparency and rationale communication. Explaining purpose behind policy reduces perceived rigidity. Recruitment improves when policies appear functional rather than ceremonial. Design influences interpretation.

4.3 Governance Structures and the Pace of Decision Making

Governance structures influence recruitment through pace as well as authority. Cybersecurity professionals operate in environments where timely decision making reduces risk. Slow processes signal vulnerability. Candidates extrapolate governance behavior during recruitment to future work conditions. Decision pace shapes commitment.

Academic governance often values deliberation and consensus. While important, excessive delay frustrates candidates. Extended silence erodes trust. Candidates interpret delay as indecision rather than care. Recruitment loses momentum quietly.

One educator accepted an offer elsewhere after months without update. The delay suggested internal fragmentation. In contrast, institutions communicating timelines retained engagement. Governance clarity preserved interest.

Institutions must balance inclusivity with decisiveness. Clear timelines and communication mitigate delay impact. Recruitment benefits from governance awareness. Pace becomes a strategic factor rather than procedural detail.

4.4 Curriculum Control and Perceived Professional Agency

Curriculum control represents a central concern for cybersecurity educators. Professionals expect autonomy in instructional design reflecting current threat landscapes. Rigid curriculum frameworks signal disconnect from disciplinary reality. Agency influences perceived value of teaching roles. Recruitment hinges on instructional freedom.

Educators describe frustration when curriculum remains frozen despite evolving risks. Teaching loses relevance under excessive constraint. Candidates evaluate whether institutions trust faculty judgment. Agency communicates respect.

Institutions vary widely in curriculum governance. Some permit instructor led evolution within outcomes. Others restrict modification tightly. Candidates interpret these differences as signals of institutional maturity. Recruitment aligns with perceived agency.

Recruitment improves when institutions articulate curriculum flexibility clearly. Transparency reduces uncertainty. Agency attracts professionals seeking meaningful contribution. Curriculum governance shapes recruitment success directly.

4.5 Hiring Processes as Signals of Institutional Coherence

Hiring processes communicate institutional coherence more clearly than formal messaging. Cybersecurity professionals evaluate consistency across human resources, academic leadership, and faculty interaction. Misalignment between these groups signals fragmentation rather than complexity. Candidates infer daily working conditions from recruitment coordination. Recruitment outcomes reflect perceived coherence.

Educators describe frustration when interview questions conflict across stakeholders. Human resources may emphasize policy compliance while faculty focus on teaching philosophy. Leadership may highlight growth ambitions without operational detail. These inconsistencies create cognitive friction. Candidates question institutional readiness.

Institutions demonstrating coordinated messaging build confidence. Clear alignment across process stages reduces uncertainty. Candidates remain engaged when communication appears intentional. Recruitment improves through coherence rather than persuasion.

Process design requires leadership oversight. Institutions assuming process functions autonomously invite misalignment. Recruitment becomes fragile under fragmented ownership. Coherence must be designed rather than assumed.

4.6 Resource Visibility and Candidate Confidence

Resource visibility influences candidate confidence significantly. Cybersecurity educators evaluate instructional support through tangible indicators. Lab environments, tooling access, and technical infrastructure signal institutional seriousness. Candidates interpret resource investment as commitment rather than promise. Visibility matters more than aspiration.

Educators recount skepticism when institutions emphasize future investment without present capability. Promises lack credibility absent demonstration. In contrast, visible resources build trust even when imperfect. Candidates value honesty regarding limitations.

Institutions benefit from transparent resource communication. Demonstrating existing labs and tools reduces perceived risk. Educators prefer clarity over optimism. Recruitment improves when resource discussion reflects reality.

Resource visibility also influences retention. Educators remain engaged when support aligns with expectation. Misalignment fuels frustration. Recruitment and retention intersect through resource honesty.

4.7 Onboarding Structures and Early Professional Integration

Onboarding structures shape early professional integration. Cybersecurity educators evaluate institutional support during initial months carefully. Weak onboarding increases isolation and doubt. Strong onboarding reinforces belonging and confidence. Early experience influences long term commitment.

Educators describe challenges navigating systems without guidance. Learning management platforms, curriculum processes, and assessment expectations require orientation. Absence of support signals indifference. Candidates interpret early neglect as cultural norm.

Institutions investing in structured onboarding observe stronger engagement. Mentorship, peer connection, and clear expectations reduce friction. Early integration accelerates instructional effectiveness. Recruitment success extends beyond offer acceptance.

Onboarding design reflects institutional values. Support signals respect for professional transition. Recruitment improves when institutions demonstrate care beyond hiring. Integration sustains commitment.

4.8 Institutional Culture and Psychological Safety

Institutional culture shapes psychological safety for cybersecurity educators. Professionals accustomed to high accountability environments value respectful challenge and open dialogue. Teaching requires vulnerability through experimentation and iteration. Psychological safety enables growth. Recruitment hinges on cultural signals.

Educators assess culture through interaction tone and responsiveness. Dismissive language or rigid hierarchy undermines confidence. Inclusive dialogue fosters trust. Candidates interpret culture quickly.

Institutions promoting psychological safety attract committed educators. Openness supports innovation and learning. Teaching thrives within supportive culture. Recruitment improves when culture aligns with professional expectations.

Culture requires intentional cultivation. Leadership behavior sets tone. Recruitment outcomes reflect cultural reality. Institutions ignoring culture undermine recruitment inadvertently.

4.9 Evaluation Practices and Perceived Fairness

Evaluation practices shape candidate perception of institutional fairness early in the recruitment process. Cybersecurity professionals expect assessment aligned with role requirements and professional reality. When evaluation focuses on irrelevant criteria, candidates infer misalignment.

Perceived unfairness erodes trust quickly. Recruitment outcomes depend on evaluation credibility.

Educators describe discomfort when interview assessments prioritize academic convention over instructional capability. Questions emphasizing publication or committee service overshadow teaching readiness. Candidates interpret this focus as signal of misplaced priorities. Interest diminishes accordingly.

Institutions improving evaluation alignment observe stronger engagement. Assessments reflecting teaching scenarios resonate with candidates. Fair evaluation reinforces legitimacy. Recruitment improves through relevance rather than rigor alone.

Evaluation design requires deliberate leadership attention. Institutions relying on inherited templates invite mismatch. Recruitment becomes fragile under misaligned assessment. Fairness must be intentional.

4.10 Flexibility, Adaptation, and Institutional Learning

Institutional flexibility influences recruitment success significantly. Cybersecurity professionals operate within environments requiring continuous adaptation. Teaching environments resistant to change signal stagnation. Candidates evaluate whether institutions learn from experience. Adaptation matters.

Educators describe frustration with institutions unwilling to adjust processes. Rigid adherence to precedent undermines confidence. Flexibility signals resilience rather than weakness. Recruitment benefits from adaptive posture.

Institutions learning from failed searches improve outcomes. Reflection informs redesign. Flexibility allows refinement of criteria and process. Recruitment becomes iterative rather than static.

Adaptive institutions attract innovative educators. Teaching thrives within learning organizations. Recruitment aligns with professional expectation. Flexibility becomes competitive advantage.

4.11 Institutional Reputation and External Signaling

Institutional reputation influences recruitment before direct engagement occurs. Cybersecurity professionals gather information through networks, conferences, and online discourse. Reputation reflects lived experience rather than marketing. External signaling shapes expectation.

Educators describe reliance on peer narratives when evaluating institutions. Positive stories attract interest. Negative stories discourage application. Reputation functions as pre screening filter.

Institutions influence reputation through consistent behavior. Fair hiring, supportive culture, and instructional quality build trust. Reputation improves through practice rather than branding. Recruitment benefits accordingly.

Ignoring reputation leaves institutions reactive. Leaders must manage external perception intentionally. Recruitment reflects reputation reality. Signals matter.

4.12 Synthesis of Institutional Influence on Recruitment Decisions

Institutional structures shape recruitment outcomes through cumulative effect. Decision environments influence interpretation, risk assessment, and commitment. Recruitment failure reflects design misalignment rather than candidate shortage. Institutions control more variables than assumed.

This chapter demonstrates recruitment depends on institutional readiness. Policies, governance, culture, and support structures interact. Alignment across these domains supports engagement. Fragmentation undermines trust.

Institutions improving recruitment must redesign environment intentionally. Leadership responsibility extends beyond process oversight. Design replaces assumption as organizing principle. Recruitment becomes sustainable.

The next chapter shifts focus toward applied leadership response. It examines how leaders translate insight into recruitment strategy. Institutional design becomes actionable. Chapter 5 moves from environment to execution.

Chapter 5: Leadership Strategies for Executing Cybersecurity Educator Recruitment

5.1 Leadership as the Primary Recruitment Signal

Leadership behavior functions as the most influential recruitment signal in cybersecurity education. Candidates evaluate leaders long before formal offers appear. How leaders communicate purpose, make decisions, and engage with uncertainty shapes perception of institutional seriousness. Recruitment success depends on leadership coherence rather than policy documentation alone. Leaders embody institutional intent through action.

Cybersecurity professionals assess leadership credibility through interaction quality. Directness, clarity, and respect for professional experience build trust quickly. Ambiguity or deflection erodes confidence. Candidates extrapolate leadership behavior into future working conditions. Recruitment hinges on leadership authenticity.

Educators describe decisive leadership as reassuring. Leaders who articulate constraints honestly foster confidence. Overpromising damages credibility. Leadership transparency matters more than aspiration.

Institutions relying on delegated recruitment without visible leadership engagement struggle. Candidates interpret absence as lack of priority. Leadership presence signals commitment. Recruitment improves when leaders participate actively.

5.2 Translating Strategy Into Role Design

Leadership strategy manifests most clearly through role design. Strategic intent fails without operational translation. Leaders define scope, expectations, and support structures. Role clarity reflects leadership discipline. Recruitment outcomes follow.

Cybersecurity educators evaluate roles as integrated systems rather than task lists. Teaching load, preparation time, service expectations, and curriculum authority interact. Leaders must balance ambition with sustainability. Poor role design repels capable candidates.

Educators recount declining roles lacking coherence. Excessive scope signaled institutional instability. Leaders misinterpreted ambition as attraction. Recruitment failed accordingly.

Effective leaders design roles reflecting respect for professional capacity. They align instructional need with realistic workload. Role design communicates seriousness. Recruitment improves through disciplined design.

5.3 Building Trust Through Recruitment Communication

Recruitment communication shapes candidate trust continuously. Leaders influence tone and consistency. Clear timelines, honest updates, and direct answers matter. Communication failure undermines otherwise strong offers.

Cybersecurity professionals value predictability. Silence increases uncertainty. Leaders who communicate delays openly maintain trust. Ambiguity triggers disengagement.

Educators describe appreciation for leaders explaining process complexity candidly. Transparency reduces frustration. Communication becomes partnership rather than transaction.

Recruitment communication reflects leadership values. Respectful dialogue attracts commitment. Leaders must treat communication as strategic tool. Recruitment improves through trust.

5.4 Aligning Search Committees With Recruitment Strategy

Search committees operationalize leadership intent during recruitment. Misalignment undermines strategy quickly. Leaders must guide committees intentionally. Recruitment success depends on committee coherence.

Cybersecurity educator searches require specialized understanding. Committees unfamiliar with discipline default to proxies. Leaders must clarify evaluation criteria. Without guidance, committees misinterpret excellence.

Educators recount confusion during interviews with inconsistent questioning. Misalignment eroded confidence. Leaders failed to prepare committees adequately. Recruitment suffered.

Effective leaders brief committees thoroughly. Shared understanding aligns evaluation. Committees reflect leadership clarity. Recruitment outcomes improve accordingly.

5.5 Decision Authority and the Cost of Indecision

Decision authority plays a decisive role in cybersecurity educator recruitment outcomes. Candidates accustomed to operational environments expect clarity regarding who holds decision power. Ambiguity surrounding authority introduces uncertainty and erodes confidence. Leaders must ensure decision rights are visible and respected throughout the recruitment process. Recruitment stalls when authority diffuses across committees without resolution.

Educators describe frustration when recommendations cycle without closure. Extended deliberation signals institutional hesitation rather than thoughtful evaluation. Candidates infer risk from unresolved authority structures. Interest diminishes as uncertainty persists. Recruitment fails quietly through delay.

Effective leaders establish decision pathways early. Committees advise while leaders decide. Clear authority accelerates momentum and preserves trust. Recruitment benefits from decisive governance.

Decisiveness does not eliminate deliberation. It frames deliberation within accountable structure. Leaders balancing inclusion and resolution attract candidates. Authority clarity underpins execution success.

5.6 Balancing Rigor and Accessibility in Candidate Evaluation

Evaluation rigor ensures instructional quality, yet excessive rigidity constrains recruitment. Leaders must balance high standards with accessibility for practitioner candidates. Evaluation frameworks should surface teaching capability without privileging academic convention unnecessarily. Recruitment improves when rigor aligns with role reality.

Cybersecurity educators often bring extensive experiential knowledge. Traditional evaluation may undervalue this experience. Leaders must design assessment reflecting instructional relevance. Teaching demonstrations and scenario discussion reveal capability more effectively.

Educators report positive experiences when evaluation centers on practice translation. These assessments validate professional identity. Rigor becomes affirming rather than exclusionary. Recruitment success follows relevance.

Leaders ensure accessibility by calibrating evaluation expectations. Clear guidance supports fairness. Rigor functions as quality assurance rather than barrier. Recruitment benefits from thoughtful balance.

5.7 Sustaining Momentum From Offer to Onboarding

Recruitment success extends beyond offer acceptance. Momentum must continue through onboarding. Leaders influence this transition significantly. Early engagement shapes commitment and confidence.

Educators describe anxiety during post offer silence. Uncertainty undermines enthusiasm. Leaders maintaining communication preserve trust. Early integration begins before first day.

Institutions supporting momentum introduce mentors early. Resource access and orientation occur promptly. Educators feel valued rather than peripheral. Commitment strengthens through continuity.

Leadership oversight ensures smooth transition. Recruitment and onboarding form continuum. Sustained momentum reduces early attrition. Execution completes through follow through.

5.8 Measuring Recruitment Success Beyond Vacancy Closure

Recruitment metrics often focus narrowly on position filling. Leaders must expand measurement to include retention and engagement. Vacancy closure alone obscures deeper outcomes. Recruitment success manifests over time.

Effective leaders track early educator experience. Satisfaction, workload balance, and instructional support matter. Feedback informs redesign. Recruitment becomes learning system.

Educators thrive when metrics align with lived experience. Leadership attention reinforces value. Recruitment strategy evolves through evidence. Success becomes sustainable.

Reframing metrics shifts leadership behavior. Recruitment improves when outcomes guide design. Measurement supports continuous improvement. Execution matures through reflection.

5.9 Leader Presence During Candidate Evaluation

Leader presence during candidate evaluation carries symbolic and practical weight. Cybersecurity professionals interpret leader involvement as evidence of institutional priority. Presence communicates seriousness more effectively than written policy or delegated process. Candidates assess whether leaders understand instructional realities through direct interaction. Recruitment outcomes respond to perceived leadership engagement.

Educators describe heightened confidence when leaders participate meaningfully in interviews. Thoughtful questions demonstrate understanding of discipline and teaching complexity. Superficial participation signals disinterest. Candidates extrapolate leader behavior into future support expectations. Presence shapes trust decisively.

Leader presence also stabilizes evaluation alignment. Leaders clarify priorities and resolve ambiguity. Committees function more cohesively under visible guidance. Recruitment benefits from consistency and direction.

Institutions treating leader presence as optional dilute recruitment impact. Strategic involvement strengthens outcomes. Presence signals stewardship rather than oversight. Recruitment succeeds when leadership remains visible.

5.10 Supporting Leader Preparedness for Cybersecurity Recruitment

Leaders require preparation to recruit cybersecurity educators effectively. Familiarity with academic hiring alone proves insufficient. Cybersecurity carries distinct professional norms and expectations. Leaders must understand these dynamics to engage candidates credibly. Preparation underpins execution.

Educators report disengagement when leaders misinterpret professional language or concerns. Credibility erodes when leaders rely on generic framing. Preparation enables meaningful dialogue. Candidates respond to informed engagement.

Institutions benefit from leader development focused on disciplinary context. Briefings, consultation, and exposure build competence. Leaders prepared for recruitment perform more confidently. Recruitment improves through preparedness.

Leader development reduces reliance on assumptions. Engagement becomes authentic rather than performative. Candidates sense preparedness quickly. Recruitment outcomes reflect leader readiness.

5.11 Recruitment as an Ongoing Leadership Practice

Recruitment should function as an ongoing leadership practice rather than episodic response. Cybersecurity educator pipelines require sustained attention. Leaders maintaining engagement between searches build institutional memory. Recruitment becomes proactive rather than reactive.

Educators often accept roles through relationships formed long before vacancies arise. Ongoing dialogue builds familiarity and trust. Leaders visible within professional communities attract interest organically. Recruitment success compounds over time.

Institutions investing in continuous recruitment outperform those relying on posting cycles. Leaders cultivate networks and maintain awareness. Recruitment readiness improves through continuity. Outcomes stabilize accordingly.

Viewing recruitment as practice shifts leadership posture. Engagement replaces urgency. Capacity replaces crisis. Recruitment becomes strategic capability.

5.12 Synthesis of Leadership Execution in Recruitment

Leadership execution determines whether recruitment insight translates into outcome. Strategy without execution fails silently. Leaders shape role design, evaluation, communication, and onboarding. Alignment across these domains produces success. Fragmentation undermines even strong intent.

This chapter demonstrates leadership influence across recruitment lifecycle. Presence, preparedness, decisiveness, and continuity matter. Recruitment reflects leadership behavior more than market conditions. Institutions control more variables than often assumed.

Effective leaders treat recruitment as stewardship. They design systems supporting educator transition. Execution aligns with professional reality. Recruitment becomes reliable.

The next chapter moves fully into applied frameworks. It provides structured tools for defining, identifying, and evaluating cybersecurity educator candidates. Chapter 6 transforms leadership execution into repeatable practice.

Chapter 6: Defining and Identifying the Cybersecurity Educator Institutions Actually Need

6.1 Moving Beyond Credentials Toward Capability

Cybersecurity educator recruitment often stalls because institutions rely too heavily on credentials as proxies for capability. Degrees and certifications provide baseline qualification but reveal little about instructional readiness. Many capable educators possess deep expertise without traditional academic markers. Institutions limiting evaluation to credentials narrow candidate pools unnecessarily. Capability emerges through practice rather than designation.

Effective cybersecurity educators demonstrate the ability to translate complexity into understanding. They contextualize technical detail within operational relevance. Instructional clarity matters more than formal pedigree. Capability reflects communication, judgment, and adaptability. Recruitment improves when institutions recognize these dimensions explicitly.

Educators often struggle to articulate capability during credential focused evaluation. Their strengths remain invisible under traditional screening. Institutions must redesign evaluation frameworks to surface instructional competence. Capability centered hiring increases alignment and retention.

Shifting focus toward capability requires leadership commitment. Credentials remain necessary but insufficient. Institutions redefining excellence gain access to broader talent. Recruitment succeeds when capability guides selection.

6.2 Instructional Readiness as a Distinct Hiring Dimension

Instructional readiness differs fundamentally from subject matter expertise. Many cybersecurity professionals possess deep knowledge without teaching preparation. Readiness reflects preparedness to design learning experiences rather than deliver information. Institutions often conflate expertise with readiness. This assumption undermines recruitment quality.

Instructional readiness includes lesson planning, assessment design, and learner engagement. It also involves comfort with facilitation and feedback. Educators describe readiness as confidence in learning design rather than content mastery. Recruitment improves when readiness receives separate evaluation.

Institutions can assess readiness through teaching demonstrations and scenario discussion. These methods reveal pedagogical thinking directly. Candidates respond positively to fair assessment. Readiness evaluation increases hiring precision.

Readiness develops through exposure and mentorship. Institutions supporting readiness growth expand candidate pools. Hiring frameworks must account for readiness potential. Recruitment improves through distinction.

6.3 Professional Credibility and Classroom Authority

Professional credibility anchors classroom authority in cybersecurity education. Students evaluate instructors based on perceived relevance and experience. Educators lacking credibility struggle to establish trust. Credibility arises from lived professional responsibility rather than titles alone. Institutions must assess credibility intentionally.

Educators describe credibility as ability to answer contextual questions confidently. Real world examples reinforce authority. Students respond to instructors who demonstrate practical judgment. Credibility sustains engagement across complex topics. Recruitment succeeds when credibility aligns with curriculum goals.

Institutions often assume credibility correlates with certification quantity. This assumption oversimplifies reality. Experience depth and decision responsibility matter more. Hiring frameworks must capture these nuances.

Credibility assessment requires narrative inquiry. Institutions must invite candidates to explain experience meaningfully. Recruitment improves when credibility receives deliberate attention. Classroom authority follows alignment.

6.4 Motivation and Commitment to Teaching Practice

Motivation influences long term educator success more than technical skill alone. Cybersecurity educators sustain engagement through purpose alignment. Teaching requires emotional investment and resilience. Institutions often underestimate motivation as a hiring variable. Recruitment suffers accordingly.

Educators describe motivation rooted in influence and contribution. Teaching aligns with desire to shape future professionals. Commitment emerges when institutions support this motivation. Recruitment improves when motivation receives evaluation.

Institutions can assess motivation through narrative questions. Candidates articulate purpose through story. Leaders gain insight into alignment. Motivation predicts retention more reliably than credentials.

Hiring frameworks incorporating motivation reduces early attrition. Educators remain engaged when purpose aligns with role design. Recruitment becomes sustainable. Motivation anchors long term success.

6.5 Translating Capability into Observable Hiring Signals

Hiring decisions improve when capability becomes observable rather than inferred. Cybersecurity educator capability must surface through structured interaction rather than credential review alone. Institutions often expect candidates to demonstrate teaching readiness without providing the opportunity to do so. This mismatch obscures strengths and reinforces bias toward traditional markers. Capability must be invited into view intentionally.

Observable capability appears through explanation, framing, and decision reasoning. Candidates who articulate why concepts matter demonstrate instructional judgment. Those who contextualize content for varied audiences reveal pedagogical awareness. These behaviors signal readiness more reliably than resumes. Recruitment improves when leaders know what to observe.

Institutions can design prompts encouraging capability demonstration. Scenario based questions elicit teaching thought processes. Teaching demonstrations provide direct evidence. Candidates respond positively to fair evaluation. Capability surfaces when structures allow it.

Leaders must train evaluators to recognize capability consistently. Without shared understanding, observation becomes subjective. Clear criteria support fairness and alignment. Recruitment succeeds through disciplined observation. Capability guided hiring produces stronger outcomes.

6.6 Designing Interviews for Surface Instructional Thinking

Interviews serve as the primary venue for evaluating instructional thinking. Traditional interviews emphasize background description rather than pedagogical reasoning. Cybersecurity educator interviews must move beyond biography. Leaders should design questions revealing how candidates think about learning. Instructional thinking predicts classroom effectiveness.

Effective interview prompts invite candidates to explain teaching decisions. Questions exploring how to introduce complex topics reveal scaffolding ability. Discussion of assessment design reveals learning priorities. Candidates demonstrate instructional maturity through reasoning rather than performance alone. Recruitment benefits from depth.

Educators describe interviews as affirming when instructional thinking receives attention. Candidates feel respected for teaching interest. This respect strengthens engagement. Interviews become dialogue rather than interrogation.

Institutions must align interview design with hiring goals. Misaligned interviews waste opportunity. Leaders should ensure questions map directly to educator dimensions. Recruitment improves through intentional interview architecture.

6.7 Using Teaching Demonstrations with Purpose and Care

Teaching demonstrations provide powerful evidence of instructional capability when designed thoughtfully. Many institutions require demonstrations without clear criteria. Candidates experience uncertainty and anxiety. Demonstrations must align with evaluation intent. Purposeful design benefits all participants.

Effective demonstrations simulate realistic teaching conditions. Topics reflect actual curriculum content. Time constraints mirror classroom reality. Candidates demonstrate pacing, engagement, and clarity. Observers evaluate relevant behaviors.

Educators report frustration when demonstrations feel performative. Artificial scenarios undermine authenticity. Clear expectations reduce stress. Candidates perform more accurately when criteria remain transparent.

Institutions should brief evaluators before demonstrations. Shared observation frameworks improve consistency. Feedback should focus on instructional behavior. Demonstrations function as learning tools. Recruitment improves when demonstrations reflect purpose.

6.8 Integrating HR and Academic Evaluation Perspectives

Effective recruitment requires integration between human resources and academic evaluation. These functions often operate independently. Misalignment produces conflicting signals. Candidates experience confusion. Recruitment outcomes suffer.

Human resources bring process discipline and compliance awareness. Academic leaders bring instructional context. Integration aligns evaluation with role reality. Shared criteria reduce friction. Recruitment improves through collaboration.

Educators describe relief when HR and faculty messaging aligns. Consistency builds trust. Candidates perceive professionalism. Engagement strengthens accordingly.

Leaders must facilitate integration intentionally. Joint planning sessions align expectations. Clear communication supports coherence. Recruitment becomes coordinated rather than fragmented. Integration anchors sustainable hiring practice.

6.9 Establishing Structured Hiring Rubrics Without Rigidity

Structured hiring rubrics improve consistency and fairness when aligned with instructional reality. Cybersecurity educator's rubrics must evaluate capability, readiness, credibility, and motivation explicitly. Overly generic rubrics collapse nuance into checklists. Effective rubrics guide judgment rather than replace it. Structure supports alignment without constraining professional evaluation.

Rubrics should define observable behaviors linked to teaching outcomes. Indicators may include clarity of explanation, contextual framing, and learner engagement strategies. Weighting should reflect program mission rather than academic tradition alone. Transparency supports candidate confidence. Recruitment improves when rubrics feel purposeful.

Educators respond positively to clear evaluation criteria. Predictability reduces anxiety and supports authentic performance. Rubrics also support committee alignment. Shared language reduces bias. Recruitment outcomes stabilize under structured evaluation.

Leaders must review rubrics regularly. Disciplinary evolution demands adjustment. Static tools lose relevance quickly. Continuous refinement sustains alignment. Rubrics function as living instruments.

6.10 Decision Frameworks for Balancing Competing Strengths

Hiring decisions often involve tradeoffs among candidate strengths. Decision frameworks help leaders navigate complexity without defaulting to familiarity. Cybersecurity educators may excel in different dimensions. Frameworks support deliberate balancing rather than reactive compromise. Recruitment benefits from explicit prioritization.

Frameworks clarify which attributes remain non-negotiable. Others allow development through onboarding. Leaders articulate acceptable gaps transparently. Candidates understand expectations more clearly. Decisions become defensible.

Educators describe appreciation for honesty regarding tradeoffs. Clear communication fosters trust. Candidates evaluate fit realistically. Recruitment improves through clarity.

Institutions using decision frameworks reduce indecision. Choices align with strategy rather than urgency. Frameworks support confidence in selection. Recruitment becomes disciplined practice.

6.11 Transition Planning from Selection to Early Success

Selection alone does not ensure instructional success. Transition planning bridges hiring and performance. Cybersecurity educators require support adapting to academic environments. Institutions often underestimate this need. Transition planning protects recruitment investment.

Effective transition includes mentorship, workload calibration, and curriculum orientation. Early clarity reduces stress and accelerates contribution. Educators feel supported rather than tested. Commitment strengthens through care.

Institutions benefit from structured early milestones. Feedback loops guide adjustment. Support demonstrates institutional readiness. Recruitment success extends into retention.

Leaders must view transition as continuation of recruitment. Early success reinforces hiring decisions. Institutions neglecting transition face avoidable attrition. Planning sustains alignment.

6.12 Synthesis of Applied Hiring Practice

This chapter translates conceptual understanding into applied hiring practice. Cybersecurity educator recruitment succeeds through intentional design rather than chance. Capability, readiness, credibility, and motivation guide selection. Structured tools support judgment without rigidity. Alignment produces outcome.

Effective hiring integrates leadership, human resources, and faculty expertise. Clear criteria, purposeful evaluation, and transition support form a coherent system. Recruitment becomes repeatable and scalable. Institutions gain confidence.

This applied framework enables immediate implementation. Leaders can adapt tools to context without losing integrity. Recruitment improves through design discipline. Practice replaces assumption.

The next chapter expands focus toward onboarding and professional development. Recruitment success matures through sustained educator growth. Chapter 7 completes the hiring lifecycle by addressing retention and development.

Chapter 7: Onboarding, Professional Development, and Retention of Cybersecurity Educators

7.1 Onboarding as a Continuation of Recruitment

Onboarding represents the final phase of recruitment rather than a separate administrative step. Cybersecurity educators enter institutions carrying expectations formed during hiring interactions. Early experiences either reinforce or undermine those expectations. Institutions treating onboarding as procedural miss an opportunity to solidify commitment. Retention begins during the first weeks rather than after the first year.

Educators often describe onboarding as a period of heightened vulnerability. New faculty navigate unfamiliar systems, cultural norms, and performance expectations simultaneously. Absence of guidance amplifies uncertainty. Effective onboarding reduces cognitive load and builds confidence. Recruitment success depends on this early stabilization.

Institutions benefit when onboarding aligns with recruitment messaging. Promised support must appear in practice. Mentorship, clear communication, and access to resources matter immediately. Consistency signals integrity. Retention improves through coherence.

Leaders must view onboarding as strategic investment. Early neglect undermines recruitment gains. Structured onboarding sustains momentum. Recruitment concludes through successful integration.

7.2 Early Role Clarity and Workload Calibration

Early role clarity influences educator satisfaction and performance. Cybersecurity educators require understanding of instructional scope, service expectations, and evaluation criteria. Ambiguity increases stress and delays effectiveness.

Institutions often assume clarity exists implicitly. Explicit communication prevents misinterpretation.

Workload calibration proves especially critical during initial terms. New educators balance course preparation, student engagement, and institutional learning. Excessive load accelerates burnout. Sustainable pacing supports instructional quality. Recruitment outcomes hinge on early workload realism.

Educators report frustration when expectations expand unexpectedly. Role creep undermines trust. Transparent workload discussion builds confidence. Leaders must calibrate ambition with capacity.

Institutions supporting gradual role expansion observe stronger retention. Early success builds momentum. Recruitment extends into performance management. Clarity anchors commitment.

7.3 Mentorship as an Anchor for Early Success

Mentorship functions as a central retention mechanism for cybersecurity educators. New faculty benefit from guidance navigating academic culture and expectations. Mentors translate institutional norms into practical understanding. This support reduces isolation and accelerates integration. Mentorship strengthens identity alignment.

Educators describe mentorship as both professional and emotional support. Access to experienced colleagues provides reassurance. Mentors validate instructional judgment and decision making. Teaching confidence grows through affirmation. Retention improves through relationship.

Institutions vary widely in mentorship quality. Informal arrangements lack consistency. Structured mentorship ensures equity. Recruitment benefits when mentorship receives intentional design.

Leaders must select mentors carefully. Compatibility matters. Mentorship requires recognition and support. Retention depends on sustained guidance. Recruitment success matures through mentorship.

7.4 Early Professional Development and Instructional Growth

Early professional development supports instructional confidence and innovation. Cybersecurity educators often possess expertise without pedagogical training. Development opportunities bridge this gap. Institutions neglecting development risk frustration. Investment signals commitment to educator success.

Effective development addresses teaching practice directly. Workshops on learning design, assessment, and engagement prove valuable. Peer observation encourages reflective improvement. Educators respond positively to relevant development. Retention improves through growth.

Institutions must avoid generic development programming. Discipline specific support enhances relevance. Cybersecurity educators require tailored resources. Alignment matters.

Professional development also supports identity integration. Educators refine teaching philosophy. Confidence stabilizes through skill acquisition. Recruitment success extends into professional growth.

7.5 Evaluation Practices That Support Growth Rather Than Attrition

Evaluation practices exert significant influence on cybersecurity educator retention. Early evaluation experiences shape perception of institutional intent. When evaluation emphasizes compliance over development, educators disengage. Growth oriented evaluation fosters confidence and improvement. Retention depends on perceived fairness and relevance.

Cybersecurity educators expect evaluation aligned with instructional reality. Metrics disconnected from classroom practice undermine credibility. Educators respond positively to feedback grounded in observable teaching behavior. Constructive dialogue supports refinement. Evaluation becomes partnership rather than judgment.

Institutions often apply uniform evaluation frameworks across disciplines. This approach overlooks cybersecurity complexity. Discipline aware evaluation increases relevance. Retention improves when evaluation reflects context.

Leaders must ensure evaluators receive preparation. Calibration reduces inconsistency. Fair evaluation reinforces trust. Recruitment gains persist through supportive assessment.

7.6 Recognition, Reward, and Professional Affirmation

Recognition functions as a powerful retention mechanism. Cybersecurity educators seek acknowledgment of instructional impact. Formal and informal recognition reinforce value. Absence of recognition signals indifference. Retention suffers quietly.

Educators describe motivation derived from visible appreciation. Student outcomes, curriculum innovation, and mentorship deserve recognition. Institutions often prioritize research output over teaching excellence. This imbalance discourages educators.

Balanced recognition frameworks strengthen commitment. Teaching focused institutions must celebrate instructional achievement. Recognition affirms professional identity. Retention improves through affirmation.

Leaders influence recognition culture directly. Consistent acknowledgment builds morale. Recognition need not require financial reward alone. Professional affirmation sustains engagement.

7.7 Sustaining Industry Connection and Professional Relevance

Sustained industry connection supports educator relevance and satisfaction. Cybersecurity evolves rapidly. Educators require continued exposure to practice. Institutions restricting external engagement risk instructional stagnation. Retention depends on relevance maintenance.

Educators value opportunities for consulting, collaboration, and professional participation. These activities enrich teaching. Institutions benefit from current curriculum content. Mutual advantage emerges.

Leaders must balance institutional policy with professional engagement. Clear guidelines support flexibility. Encouraging connection signals respect. Retention improves through relevance support.

Industry connection also strengthens recruitment reputation. Institutions known for relevance attract talent. Educator satisfaction reinforces credibility. Retention and recruitment align.

7.8 Creating Career Pathways for Cybersecurity Educators

Career pathways influence long term retention significantly. Cybersecurity educators seek growth beyond initial appointment. Institutions often lack clear advancement models. Ambiguity discourages commitment. Retention suffers through stagnation.

Educators desire pathways reflecting instructional leadership. Curriculum development, program coordination, and mentorship offer progression. Recognition of these roles matters. Career clarity sustains motivation.

Institutions benefit from diversified advancement models. Not all educators pursue research leadership. Teaching focused pathways increase stability. Retention improves through opportunity.

Leaders must articulate pathways transparently. Career planning begins early. Clear progression supports engagement. Recruitment success matures into retention.

7.9 Psychological Contract and Long-Term Commitment

Cybersecurity educator retention depends heavily on the psychological contract formed between educator and institution. This contract reflects perceived promises rather than written agreements. Educators assess whether institutional behavior aligns with expectations set during recruitment and onboarding. Misalignment erodes trust gradually rather than immediately. Commitment weakens through accumulation of small disappointments.

Educators describe heightened sensitivity to inconsistency during early years. Promised autonomy, support, or flexibility must appear in practice. When reality diverges, confidence declines. Educators reinterpret institutional intent through lived experience. Retention hinges on consistency.

Institutions strengthen psychological contracts through follow-through. Leaders must honor commitments explicitly. Transparent communication mitigates unavoidable constraints. Trust sustains engagement.

Recruitment success matures into retention when psychological contracts remain intact. Institutions ignoring this dimension face attrition despite competitive hiring. Commitment grows through integrity. Retention reflects promise fulfillment.

7.10 Preventing Burnout Through Structural Support

Burnout presents a significant retention risk for cybersecurity educators. Teaching demands emotional labor alongside cognitive effort. Institutions often underestimate this load. Structural support mitigates burnout more effectively than individual resilience. Retention improves through systemic design.

Educators describe burnout emerging from sustained overload rather than crisis. Excessive preparation, service, and advising accumulate strain. Without adjustment, enthusiasm declines. Institutions must monitor workload actively. Prevention requires intervention.

Structural supports include workload review, schedule flexibility, and resource access. Leaders must normalize adjustment rather than endurance. Support signals care. Educators remain engaged when institutions respond.

Burnout prevention sustains instructional quality. Retention protects recruitment investment. Institutions designing for sustainability outperform reactive peers. Support underpins long term success.

7.11 Continuous Feedback and Institutional Learning

Continuous feedback supports retention through mutual learning. Cybersecurity educators value voice and responsiveness. Institutions benefiting from feedback evolve more effectively. Silence breeds disengagement. Feedback loops anchor engagement.

Educators describe appreciation for regular dialogue with leadership. Feedback validates experience and surfaces issues early. Institutions responding constructively build trust. Learning becomes shared.

Feedback mechanisms must be structured and safe. Anonymous input supports honesty. Action demonstrates seriousness. Retention improves through responsiveness.

Institutions treating feedback as strategic asset adapt more quickly. Recruitment and retention align through learning. Engagement deepens through dialogue. Continuous feedback sustains alignment.

7.12 Synthesis of Retention as Strategic Capability

Retention functions as a strategic capability rather than administrative outcome. Cybersecurity educator retention reflects institutional design, leadership behavior, and cultural integrity. Recruitment success proves temporary without retention support. Institutions must integrate retention into strategy deliberately. Capability emerges through alignment.

This chapter demonstrates retention begins with onboarding and extends through career development. Psychological contracts, burnout prevention, feedback, and growth pathways interact. Retention reflects system coherence rather than individual resilience. Leaders influence outcomes directly.

Institutions mastering retention stabilize programs and strengthen reputation. Educators remain engaged and effective. Recruitment improves as reputation grows. Retention and recruitment reinforce each other.

The next chapter transitions toward organizational maturity and scaling. It examines how institutions institutionalize effective recruitment and retention practices. Chapter 8 focuses on sustainability and long-term workforce strategy.

Chapter 8: Scaling Recruitment and Retention into Institutional Maturity

8.1 From Isolated Success to Repeatable Capability

Many institutions achieve occasional success in recruiting strong cybersecurity educators. These successes often result from exceptional circumstances rather than systematic design. Without structure, success remains fragile and difficult to reproduce. Institutional maturity emerges when recruitment and retention become repeatable capabilities rather than isolated wins. Scaling requires intentional codification of practice.

Cybersecurity educator recruitment involves complex judgment across identity, timing, and institutional fit. When this knowledge remains tacit, it disappears with leadership turnover. Institutions must capture effective practices explicitly. Documentation, shared language, and training preserve learning. Maturity depends on institutional memory.

Leaders play a critical role in moving from intuition to system. Reflecting on successful hires reveals patterns worth formalizing. These patterns inform future decision making. Scaling begins with deliberate analysis of what worked and why.

Institutions failing to codify success regress over time. Each search begins from scratch. Effort increases while outcomes stagnate. Maturity replaces reinvention with refinement. Recruitment stabilizes through repetition.

8.2 Institutionalizing Recruitment Knowledge and Practice

Institutional maturity requires recruitment knowledge to reside beyond individual leaders. Human resources, academic leadership, and faculty must share understanding. Common frameworks align interpretation across roles. Recruitment improves when language and criteria remain consistent. Knowledge institutionalization reduces variability.

Cybersecurity educator recruitment benefits from shared mental models. Clear definitions of capability, readiness, and credibility guide evaluation. Training search participants supports alignment. Institutions relying on informal understanding invite inconsistency. Maturity demands explicit knowledge transfer.

Educators describe confidence when processes feel familiar across searches. Predictability signals professionalism. Institutions known for consistent practice attract candidates. Reputation strengthens through reliability.

Leaders must invest in onboarding for those conducting searches. Recruitment practice requires development like any other capability. Institutions neglecting this investment remain dependent on personalities. Maturity emerges through shared competence.

8.3 Scaling Without Diluting Quality

Scaling recruitment introduces risk of quality dilution. Institutions expanding programs may prioritize speed over fit. Cybersecurity education suffers under misaligned growth. Maturity balances expansion with integrity. Quality preservation requires discipline.

Educators describe strain when rapid hiring overwhelms onboarding and support. New faculty struggle without infrastructure. Retention declines as quality erodes. Scaling must consider capacity alongside demand.

Institutions maintain quality by preserving evaluation rigor while improving efficiency. Streamlined processes need not sacrifice judgment. Clear frameworks support speed with integrity. Recruitment succeeds when pace aligns with preparedness.

Leaders must resist pressure to compromise standards. Short term gains undermine long term stability. Mature institutions expand thoughtfully. Scaling reflects strategy rather than urgency.

8.4 Workforce Planning as a Strategic Function

Long term cybersecurity educator sustainability depends on workforce planning. Reactive hiring responds to vacancy rather than trajectory. Strategic planning anticipates need based on enrollment, curriculum evolution, and retirement patterns. Institutions treating workforce planning as strategic gain advantage. Maturity emerges through foresight.

Workforce planning requires collaboration across units. Academic leaders forecast program direction. Human resources assess labor dynamics. Leadership aligns planning with institutional mission. Recruitment shifts from response to preparation.

Educators benefit from stable planning environments. Predictability supports career commitment. Institutions reduce crisis hiring and burnout. Planning stabilizes culture.

Without workforce planning, institutions remain vulnerable to disruption. Unexpected departures create urgency. Quality suffers under pressure. Strategic planning transforms recruitment into sustainable practice. Maturity depends on anticipation.

8.5 Governance Models That Support Sustainable Recruitment

Governance models determine whether recruitment capability persists beyond individual leadership tenure.

Cybersecurity educator recruitment suffers when governance relies on informal influence rather than defined authority. Clear governance structures align responsibility, accountability, and decision rights. Institutions with mature governance avoid ambiguity during leadership transition. Sustainability depends on structural clarity.

Educators perceive governance quality through consistency of experience. Stable processes signal institutional seriousness. Fragmented governance produces uneven outcomes. Recruitment quality fluctuates under unclear authority. Governance design directly influences candidate confidence.

Effective governance distributes responsibility while preserving decisiveness. Committees advise within defined scope. Leaders retain resolution authority. Recruitment improves when governance balances inclusion and clarity.

Institutions must document governance roles explicitly. New leaders inherit functioning systems rather than improvisation. Governance continuity protects recruitment quality. Maturity rests on structural integrity.

8.6 Measuring Recruitment and Retention Maturity

Institutional maturity requires measurement beyond vacancy metrics. Leaders must evaluate recruitment capability as system performance. Metrics should reflect alignment, retention, and educator satisfaction. Measurement informs improvement rather than compliance. Mature institutions measure what matters.

Effective metrics include time to productivity, early retention, and instructional effectiveness. Educator feedback provides qualitative insight. These measures reveal system health. Institutions relying solely on headcount miss warning signals.

Measurement supports accountability across functions. Human resources, leadership, and faculty share responsibility. Data guides refinement. Recruitment evolves through evidence.

Institutions must review metrics regularly. Static dashboards lose relevance. Adaptive measurement reflects institutional learning. Maturity emerges through feedback informed governance.

8.7 Leadership Transition and Institutional Memory

Leadership transitions pose risk to recruitment continuity. Institutional memory often resides within individuals rather than systems. When leaders depart, knowledge evaporates. Recruitment capability regresses. Maturity requires preservation beyond tenure.

Educators experience disruption during leadership change. Inconsistent practice undermines trust. Institutions maintaining continuity retain confidence. Documentation and training preserve memory.

Succession planning supports recruitment stability. Incoming leaders receive orientation to recruitment frameworks. Continuity reduces re-learning. Recruitment performance stabilizes.

Institutions investing in memory outperform those relying on charisma. Systems endure while personalities change. Maturity reflects resilience. Recruitment remains reliable across transition.

8.8 Synthesis of Institutional Maturity in Recruitment

Institutional maturity reflects the ability to sustain recruitment and retention capability over time. Recruitment evolves from ad hoc effort to strategic system. Governance, measurement, planning, and memory interact. Maturity emerges through integration rather than isolated improvement.

This chapter demonstrates scaling requires intentional design. Institutions control many variables influencing outcome. Leadership behavior, structure, and learning shape success. Recruitment stability becomes achievable.

Mature institutions attract educators through reputation and reliability. Retention improves as systems support growth. Recruitment and retention reinforce each other. Capability compounds over time.

The next chapter concludes the book with strategic guidance for implementation. It synthesizes lessons into actionable steps. Chapter 9 moves from maturity to stewardship and long-term leadership responsibility.

Chapter 9: Executive Stewardship and the Long-Term Future of Cybersecurity Educator Recruitment

9.1 Recruitment as a Stewardship Responsibility

Cybersecurity educator recruitment ultimately reflects executive stewardship rather than operational execution alone. Senior leaders determine whether recruitment receives sustained attention or episodic concern. Stewardship requires long term perspective beyond immediate vacancy pressure. Leaders shape institutional posture through priority and example. Recruitment success follows leadership intent over time.

Executives influence recruitment indirectly through resource allocation and governance design. Their decisions signal seriousness to internal stakeholders. When recruitment aligns with institutional mission, commitment strengthens. Stewardship integrates recruitment into strategic planning. Institutions mature when leaders treat recruitment as enduring responsibility.

Educators respond to visible stewardship. Confidence grows when leadership articulates long-term commitment. Recruitment improves through stability rather than urgency. Stewardship anchors trust.

Without stewardship, recruitment fragments. Short term focus undermines consistency. Institutions cycle through repeated failure. Stewardship transforms recruitment into institutional capability.

9.2 Sequencing Implementation for Sustainable Change

Effective implementation requires thoughtful sequencing rather than simultaneous overhaul. Institutions often attempt to change multiple variables at once. This approach overwhelms capacity and dilutes focus. Sequencing enables learning and adjustment. Sustainable change unfolds deliberately.

Leaders should begin with diagnostic clarity. Understanding current recruitment weaknesses guides action. Early wins build confidence. Incremental implementation allows refinement. Sequencing aligns change with institutional readiness.

Educators benefit from gradual improvement rather than disruption. Clear communication supports transition. Institutions maintain momentum through pacing. Recruitment systems stabilize through iteration.

Sequencing requires patience and discipline. Leaders must resist pressure for immediate transformation. Sustainable change favors steady progress. Recruitment improves through sequencing rather than acceleration.

9.3 Accountability and Ownership at the Executive Level

Accountability ensures recruitment initiatives persist beyond planning. Executive ownership clarifies responsibility. Without ownership, initiatives drift. Leaders must define who remains accountable for outcomes. Accountability sustains focus.

Cybersecurity educator recruitment crosses functional boundaries. Executive oversight integrates effort across units. Ownership prevents diffusion. Clear accountability aligns incentives. Recruitment benefits from decisive leadership.

Educators interpret accountability through follow-through. Promises require execution. Leaders demonstrating accountability build credibility. Recruitment trust deepens.

Institutions lacking executive accountability repeat mistakes. Responsibility shifts without resolution. Recruitment stagnates. Ownership transforms intent into outcome.

9.4 Ethical Responsibility to the Future Workforce

Recruiting cybersecurity educators carries ethical responsibility. Educators shape future professionals entrusted with societal protection. Institutions influence workforce readiness through teaching quality. Ethical stewardship demands investment in educator capability. Recruitment decisions affect public interest.

Executives must consider long-term impact beyond institutional metrics. Educator quality influences graduate competence. Ethical responsibility extends to students and employers. Recruitment becomes moral obligation.

Educators align with institutions demonstrating ethical awareness. Purpose driven leadership attracts commitment. Recruitment improves through values alignment. Ethics anchor strategy.

Ignoring ethical dimension reduces recruitment to transaction. Institutions lose meaning. Stewardship restores purpose. Recruitment gains depth.

9.5 Embedding Recruitment into Long Term Institutional Strategy

Sustainable cybersecurity educator recruitment requires explicit integration into long term institutional strategy. Recruitment must align with mission, growth planning, and workforce development priorities. When recruitment remains peripheral, it competes unsuccessfully with short-term demands. Strategic embedding ensures continuity across leadership cycles. Institutions mature when recruitment receives the same attention as enrollment and finance.

Executives influence strategic embedding through planning documents and governance structures. Explicit inclusion elevates recruitment from operational concern to strategic imperative. This elevation shapes behavior across units. Recruitment outcomes improve through alignment.

Educators respond positively to institutions demonstrating strategic intent. Long term planning signals stability and seriousness. Recruitment becomes attractive rather than uncertain. Strategic integration anchors trust.

Without embedding, recruitment remains reactive. Institutions respond to crisis rather than opportunity. Long term capability fails to develop. Strategy transforms recruitment into enduring function.

9.6 Building Leadership Capacity for Ongoing Stewardship

Stewardship depends on leadership capacity rather than individual effort. Institutions must prepare leaders to understand and execute recruitment responsibilities. Leadership development supports continuity and competence. Without preparation, stewardship weakens over time. Capacity building sustains recruitment quality.

Executives benefit from exposure to recruitment frameworks and decision models. Understanding candidate motivation and institutional signals improves judgment. Leaders equipped with shared language collaborate more effectively. Recruitment improves through leadership competence.

Educators interpret leadership capability through interaction quality. Informed engagement builds confidence. Leadership development reduces reliance on intuition alone. Recruitment benefits from preparation.

Institutions investing in leadership capacity outperform peers. Stewardship persists beyond tenure. Recruitment stability follows competence. Capacity anchors long term success.

9.7 Reflection, Learning, and Continuous Improvement

Continuous improvement anchors recruitment stewardship. Institutions must reflect on outcomes honestly. Learning requires willingness to examine failure as well as success. Reflection informs adaptation. Recruitment systems evolve through feedback.

Executives must model reflective practice. Open discussion of outcomes reduces defensiveness. Learning cultures support improvement. Recruitment benefits from transparency.

Educators value institutions willing to learn. Responsiveness builds trust. Continuous improvement signals respect for professional input. Recruitment strengthens through adaptation.

Without reflection, institutions repeat ineffective patterns. Improvement stagnates. Stewardship requires learning orientation. Recruitment matures through reflection.

9.8 Closing Synthesis and Call to Stewardship

Cybersecurity educator recruitment represents a defining leadership responsibility. Institutions shape future workforce quality through recruitment decisions. Stewardship demands intentional design, sustained attention, and ethical commitment. Leaders control more variables than often assumed. Recruitment success reflects leadership maturity.

This book has traced recruitment from diagnosis through execution and sustainability. It has demonstrated recruitment failure reflects misalignment rather than scarcity. Institutions equipped with insight can redesign outcomes. Stewardship transforms challenge into capability.

Executives, academic leaders, and human resources professionals share responsibility. Collaboration supports coherence. Recruitment improves through collective stewardship. Leadership determines trajectory.

The future of cybersecurity education depends on stewardship enacted today. Institutions willing to invest thoughtfully will thrive. Recruitment becomes strength rather than liability. Stewardship secures the field.

Appendix A Cybersecurity Educator Capability Assessment Framework

Purpose

This framework enables hiring teams to evaluate cybersecurity educator candidates beyond credentials, focusing on instructional capability, readiness, credibility, and motivation.

Core Evaluation Domains

1. **Instructional Capability**
   Evaluates the candidate's ability to translate complex cybersecurity concepts into understandable, relevant learning experiences. Evidence includes clarity of explanation, contextual framing, and responsiveness to learner needs. Capability reflects teaching judgment rather than content recitation. Candidates demonstrate this through narrative explanation and teaching scenarios. This domain prioritizes effectiveness over pedigree.

2. **Instructional Readiness**
   Assesses preparedness to design courses, assessments, and learning activities. Readiness differs from expertise and reflects confidence in teaching practice. Indicators include lesson planning ability, assessment reasoning, and learner engagement strategies. Readiness may be fully developed or emerging. Institutions should distinguish readiness gaps that can be supported from capability gaps that cannot.

3. **Professional Credibility**
   Measures alignment between professional experience and instructional authority. Credibility derives from lived responsibility, decision making, and relevance to curriculum scope. Candidates demonstrate

credibility through applied examples and reflective judgment. Certifications alone do not establish credibility. This domain anchors classroom trust.

4. **Motivation and Commitment**
   Evaluates alignment between candidate purpose and teaching role. Motivation predicts retention and engagement. Candidates articulate motivation through narrative reflection rather than statements of interest. Commitment appears in long-term orientation toward education. This domain safeguards sustainability.

Appendix B Structured Interview Question Bank

Instructional Capability

- Describe how you would introduce a complex cybersecurity topic to students with limited technical background.
- Explain a time you adapted your explanation after realizing learners were confused.

Instructional Readiness

- Walk us through how you would design a lesson on incident response decision making.
- How do you assess whether students truly understand applied risk concepts?

Professional Credibility

- Describe a professional experience you frequently draw upon when teaching.
- How do you connect real world decision making to academic learning outcomes?

Motivation and Commitment

- What draws you to teaching cybersecurity at this stage of your career?
- How do you define long-term impact as an educator?

Appendix C Teaching Demonstration Evaluation Guide

Purpose
Provides a consistent structure for evaluating teaching demonstrations fairly and meaningfully.

Evaluation Dimensions

- Clarity and structure of explanation
- Relevance and contextual framing
- Learner engagement strategies
- Pacing and adaptability
- Professional confidence and credibility

Guidance for Committees
Evaluators should focus on teaching behavior rather than performance polish. Demonstrations simulate real teaching conditions rather than staged delivery. Feedback should reference observable behaviors. Consistency across evaluators is essential.

Appendix D Hiring Decision Alignment Matrix

Purpose
Supports balanced decision making when candidates exhibit differing strengths.

Decision Categories

- Non-negotiable attributes aligned to program mission
- Attributes suitable for development through onboarding
- Attributes misaligned with institutional needs

This matrix prevents defaulting to familiarity or urgency. It enables transparent justification of hiring decisions. Leaders retain authority while benefiting from structured input.

Appendix E Onboarding and Retention Checklist

First 90 Days

- Assigned faculty mentor
- Clear teaching load and expectations
- Access to curriculum and learning systems
- Introduction to evaluation criteria

First Year

- Pedagogical development support
- Workload review and calibration
- Industry engagement discussion
- Feedback loop with leadership

This checklist treats onboarding as a continuation of recruitment rather than an administrative formality.

Appendix F Board-Level Briefing

Title

Building Sustainable Cybersecurity Educator Capacity: A Strategic Imperative for Institutional Leadership

Executive Summary

Cybersecurity educator recruitment represents a structural risk for higher education institutions. Persistent faculty shortages undermine instructional quality, program stability, employer confidence, and workforce readiness. Traditional explanations focusing on labor scarcity or compensation fail to account for recurring recruitment failure. Evidence indicates misalignment between institutional design and professional decision making as the primary cause.

This briefing synthesizes findings from a comprehensive research-based analysis of cybersecurity educator recruitment. It demonstrates that successful recruitment depends on leadership stewardship, institutional readiness, and intentional design rather than market conditions alone. Cybersecurity professionals approach teaching decisions through identity, timing, risk assessment, and trust evaluation. Institutions that ignore these dynamics experience repeated hiring failure regardless of effort.

The research identifies four educator dimensions essential for effective hiring: instructional capability, instructional readiness, professional credibility, and motivation. Institutions relying exclusively on credentials misidentify talent and constrain applicant pools. Recruitment success improves when evaluation frameworks surface these dimensions directly through structured interviews, teaching demonstrations, and narrative inquiry.

Retention emerges as inseparable from recruitment. Early onboarding, workload calibration, mentorship, and professional development determine whether recruitment gains persist. Institutions that treat hiring as transactional experience early attrition. Those that treat recruitment as a lifecycle responsibility stabilize faculty communities and strengthen program reputation.

At the executive level, recruitment must be embedded into long-term strategy. Governance clarity, leadership accountability, workforce planning, and continuous learning distinguish mature institutions from reactive ones. Recruitment success compounds over time when institutional memory and capability are preserved across leadership transitions.

Board-Level Implications

- Cybersecurity educator recruitment is a strategic risk and opportunity
- Leadership behavior influences recruitment outcomes more than labor conditions
- Sustainable recruitment requires investment in systems, not episodic searches
- Retention protection preserves recruitment investment
- Institutions that steward educator capacity strengthen workforce outcomes

Recommended Actions

- Adopt capability-based hiring frameworks
- Integrate recruitment into institutional strategic planning
- Fund onboarding and professional development as retention safeguards

- Hold executive leadership accountable for recruitment outcomes
- Treat educator capacity as critical infrastructure

Appendix G Search Committee Training Module

(Operational Deployment Package)

This module can be delivered as a **90-minute training** or **self-paced onboarding** for committee members.

Module Title

Hiring Cybersecurity Educators for Instructional Excellence and Retention

Module Objectives

Participants will be able to:

- Understand how cybersecurity professionals evaluate teaching roles
- Apply capability-based evaluation consistently
- Avoid common screening and interview failure patterns
- Align committee evaluation with institutional strategy

Module Section 1 — Why Cybersecurity Hiring Is Different

Cybersecurity is a practice-formed discipline. Many effective educators come from professional environments rather than academic pipelines. Committees relying solely on academic markers unintentionally exclude high-quality candidates. Understanding professional identity improves evaluation accuracy. This module reframes hiring expectations accordingly.

Module Section 2 — The Four Evaluation Dimensions

Committees evaluate candidates across four domains:

- Instructional capability

- Instructional readiness
- Professional credibility
- Motivation and commitment

Each domain reflects observable behavior rather than assumed qualification. Committee members are trained to recognize evidence in narrative responses and teaching demonstrations.

Module Section 3 — Interviewing for Instructional Thinking

Committees are trained to:

- Ask scenario-based questions
- Listen for pedagogical reasoning
- Evaluate clarity and contextual framing
- Avoid overvaluing biography

Interview quality predicts hiring quality.

Module Section 4 — Teaching Demonstration Evaluation

Committees learn to:

- Evaluate teaching behavior, not polish
- Focus on clarity, engagement, and relevance
- Use shared observation criteria
- Provide consistent feedback

Demonstrations are assessment tools, not performance theater.

Module Section 5 — Decision Alignment and Bias Control

Committees practice:

- Using decision matrices
- Identifying non-negotiable attributes
- Distinguishing developable gaps from misalignment
- Documenting rationale transparently

This prevents urgency and familiarity bias.

Module Section 6 — Committee Responsibilities Post-Hire

Recruitment responsibility does not end at offer acceptance. Committees:

- Support onboarding continuity
- Provide early feedback loops
- Inform process improvement

Hiring success includes early retention.

Appendix H 90-Minute Search Committee Facilitation Guide

Cybersecurity Educator Recruitment

This guide is written so any Dean, HR Partner, or Provost's Office can run it without improvisation.

Session Overview

Audience:
Search committee members, HR partners, academic leadership

Duration:
90 minutes

Format:
Facilitated workshop (in person or virtual)

Purpose:
To align search committee members on how to evaluate cybersecurity educator candidates effectively, fairly, and consistently, using the frameworks established in Chapters 6 and 7.

Learning Outcomes

By the end of the session, participants will be able to:

- Understand why cybersecurity educator hiring differs from traditional faculty hiring
- Apply the four-dimension evaluation framework consistently
- Conduct interviews that surface instructional capability rather than credentials alone
- Evaluate teaching demonstrations reliably
- Make aligned, defensible hiring recommendations

Agenda at a Glance (90 Minutes)

Time	Segment
0–10 min	Context and purpose
10–25 min	Why cybersecurity educator hiring fails
25–45 min	The four-dimension evaluation framework
45–60 min	Interviewing for instructional thinking
60–75 min	Teaching demonstration evaluation
75–85 min	Decision alignment and bias control
85–90 min	Close and committee responsibilities

Facilitation Script and Content

0–10 Minutes: Context and Purpose

Facilitator Talking Points

Cybersecurity educator recruitment is not failing because of talent scarcity alone. It fails when institutions evaluate candidates using criteria misaligned with how cybersecurity professionals decide to teach. This session establishes a shared evaluation language so the committee can assess candidates consistently and fairly. The goal is not to lower standards, but to apply the right standards.

Key Framing Rule for the Session

The committee evaluates instructional effectiveness and long-term fit, not academic pedigree alone.

10–25 Minutes: Why Cybersecurity Educator Hiring Is Different

Facilitator Explanation

Cybersecurity is a practice-formed discipline. Many highly effective educators come from industry, government, or military roles where teaching occurred informally through mentoring and training. Traditional faculty screening often fails to capture this capability.

Discussion Prompt (5 minutes)
Ask participants:

- What assumptions do we usually make about "qualified faculty"?
- Which of those assumptions may not apply to cybersecurity?

Key Takeaway

If the committee relies exclusively on degrees, publications, or prior academic titles, it will unintentionally exclude strong candidates.

25–45 Minutes: The Four-Dimension Evaluation Framework

Introduce the framework slowly and deliberately.

1. Instructional Capability

Ability to explain, contextualize, and adapt cybersecurity concepts for learners.

2. Instructional Readiness

Preparedness to design lessons, assessments, and learning experiences.

3. Professional Credibility

Lived experience that establishes classroom authority and relevance.

4. Motivation and Commitment

Alignment with teaching purpose and long-term educator identity.

Facilitator Guidance

No candidate will score equally across all four dimensions. The committee's task is to balance strengths, not search for perfection.

Mini-Exercise (10 minutes)
Present a short hypothetical candidate profile and ask:

- Which dimensions are strongest?
- Which are developable?
- Which are misaligned?

45–60 Minutes: Interviewing for Instructional Thinking

Facilitator Talking Points

Traditional interviews emphasize biography. Effective interviews surface how candidates think about teaching.

Effective Question Types

- "How would you introduce…"
- "How do you know students understand…"
- "Describe how you adapt when learners struggle…"

What to Listen For

- Clarity of explanation
- Awareness of learners
- Ability to scaffold complexity
- Reflection on teaching decisions

Red Flag Reminder
Long technical answers without learner framing indicate misalignment.

60–75 Minutes: Teaching Demonstration Evaluation

Facilitator Guidance

Teaching demonstrations are not performances. They are diagnostic tools.

Committee Evaluation Focus

- Structure and clarity
- Relevance to learners
- Engagement strategies
- Pacing and adaptability
- Professional confidence

What Not to Evaluate

- Presentation polish alone
- Entertainment value
- Memorization

Consistency Rule
All evaluators must use the same observation criteria and record evidence, not impressions.

75–85 Minutes: Decision Alignment and Bias Control

Facilitator Talking Points

Hiring decisions fail when urgency or familiarity overrides alignment.

Committee Practices

- Identify non-negotiable attributes first
- Separate developable gaps from misalignment
- Document rationale clearly

Bias Check
Ask explicitly:

- Are we favoring familiarity over effectiveness?
- Are we penalizing nontraditional career paths?

85–90 Minutes: Close and Responsibilities

Final Framing

The committee's responsibility extends beyond selection. Early alignment supports onboarding and retention. Strong hiring decisions protect program quality and institutional reputation.

Close With This Statement

A well-aligned hire reduces recruitment burden for years. A misaligned hire creates it immediately.

Accreditation-Aligned Appendix

Recruitment and Retention as Institutional Effectiveness Evidence

This appendix can be attached to self-study reports, program reviews, or accreditation narratives.

Purpose

To demonstrate how cybersecurity educator recruitment and retention align with institutional effectiveness, faculty qualification, and student learning standards.

Alignment Areas (Generic, Accreditor-Neutral)

Faculty Qualifications

- Capability-based hiring validates instructional competence
- Professional experience aligned to curriculum outcomes
- Documented evaluation criteria and rubrics

Evidence Examples:
Hiring rubrics, interview protocols, teaching demonstration evaluations

Institutional Effectiveness

- Recruitment metrics beyond vacancy fill
- Retention and early productivity tracking
- Continuous improvement through feedback loops

Evidence Examples:
Retention data, onboarding evaluations, faculty surveys

Academic Quality and Student Learning

- Stable faculty supports curriculum coherence
- Professional credibility enhances applied learning
- Instructional readiness improves assessment outcomes

Evidence Examples:
Curriculum maps, assessment reports, employer feedback

Governance and Leadership

- Clear decision authority in hiring
- Leadership accountability for recruitment outcomes
- Succession planning preserves institutional memory

Evidence Examples:
Governance documents, committee charters, leadership role definitions

Strategic Planning

- Workforce planning aligned to enrollment and program growth
- Recruitment embedded into institutional strategy
- Long-term faculty capacity management

Evidence Examples:
Strategic plans, workforce forecasts, budget alignment

Accreditation Narrative Statement (Ready to Use)

The institution approaches cybersecurity educator recruitment as a strategic and continuous process aligned with instructional quality, institutional effectiveness, and workforce sustainability. Faculty are evaluated using structured, capability-based frameworks that assess instructional readiness, professional credibility, and motivation alongside formal qualifications. Recruitment is integrated with onboarding, professional development, and retention practices to ensure instructional continuity and student success. Leadership oversight, governance clarity, and continuous improvement mechanisms support long-term faculty capacity and program stability.

DEAC Accreditation Aligned Appendix

Recruitment and Retention of Cybersecurity Educators

This appendix is written in **DEAC-aligned language** and can be inserted directly into:

- Self-evaluation reports
- Substantive change documentation
- Program review narratives

Alignment With DEAC Standards (Narrative Format)

Faculty Qualifications and Sufficiency (DEAC Standards on Faculty)

The institution ensures cybersecurity faculty possess qualifications appropriate to the level and scope of instruction, combining formal education with relevant professional experience. Faculty selection emphasizes instructional capability, professional credibility, and readiness to teach applied cybersecurity content. Structured hiring rubrics and teaching demonstrations are used to validate instructional effectiveness. This approach supports faculty sufficiency and instructional quality across programs.

Evidence

- Faculty hiring rubrics
- Teaching demonstration evaluation forms
- Professional experience documentation

Educational Quality and Student Achievement

Stable and qualified cybersecurity faculty contribute directly to educational quality and student learning outcomes. The institution integrates recruitment, onboarding, and professional development to support instructional consistency. Faculty expertise aligns with curriculum requirements and workforce expectations. Continuous evaluation ensures teaching effectiveness supports student achievement.

Evidence

- Curriculum alignment maps
- Course evaluation summaries
- Student learning assessment results

Institutional Effectiveness and Continuous Improvement

Cybersecurity educator recruitment and retention are incorporated into institutional effectiveness processes. The institution monitors hiring outcomes, early retention, and instructional performance. Feedback mechanisms inform process improvement. Recruitment practices are reviewed and refined regularly to support institutional mission and educational effectiveness.

Evidence

- Recruitment and retention metrics
- Faculty feedback summaries
- Continuous improvement documentation

Administrative Capacity and Oversight

Leadership oversight ensures cybersecurity educator recruitment aligns with institutional goals. Clear decision authority and governance structures support consistent hiring practices. Executive leadership remains accountable for recruitment outcomes. Institutional memory and documentation preserve recruitment capability across leadership transitions.

Evidence

- Governance documents
- Leadership role descriptions
- Recruitment process documentation

Strategic Planning and Workforce Sustainability

The institution incorporates cybersecurity faculty workforce planning into strategic planning. Anticipated enrollment growth, curriculum evolution, and faculty succession are considered. Recruitment is proactive rather than reactive. This approach supports long-term program stability and compliance with DEAC expectations.

Evidence

- Strategic plan excerpts
- Workforce planning projections
- Budget alignment documentation

DEAC-Ready Summary Statement (Insertable)

The institution approaches cybersecurity educator recruitment and retention as a strategic function aligned with instructional quality, institutional effectiveness, and workforce sustainability. Faculty hiring emphasizes instructional capability, professional credibility, and readiness to teach applied cybersecurity content. Recruitment processes are integrated with onboarding, professional development, and evaluation to support student learning outcomes and long-term faculty stability. Leadership oversight and continuous improvement mechanisms ensure compliance with DEAC standards and institutional mission.

Regional Accreditation Aligned Appendix

Cybersecurity Educator Recruitment and Retention as Institutional Effectiveness

Purpose of This Appendix

This appendix documents how the institution's cybersecurity educator recruitment, onboarding, professional development, and retention practices align with regional accreditation expectations related to:

- Faculty qualifications and sufficiency
- Educational quality and student learning
- Institutional effectiveness and continuous improvement
- Governance, leadership, and administrative capacity
- Strategic planning and sustainability

The practices described reflect a systematic, evidence-based approach to faculty workforce development consistent with regional accreditation standards.

Alignment Overview by Common Regional Standards

Language intentionally mirrors regional reviewer expectations and avoids program-specific jargon.

I. Faculty Qualifications and Sufficiency

(HLC Criterion 3 | MSCHE Standard III | SACSCOC Standard 6 | NECHE Standard 3 | WSCUC CFR 2)

Narrative Alignment

The institution ensures cybersecurity educators are qualified through a combination of appropriate academic preparation, relevant professional experience, and demonstrated instructional capability. Faculty hiring emphasizes not only formal credentials, but also instructional readiness and professional credibility aligned to course and program learning outcomes.

Structured hiring frameworks, including capability-based rubrics, scenario-based interviews, and teaching demonstrations, are used to validate instructional effectiveness. This approach ensures faculty are sufficient in number, qualified for assigned responsibilities, and capable of supporting student learning across delivery modalities.

Faculty sufficiency is monitored through enrollment projections, workload analysis, and retention tracking to ensure instructional continuity and program stability.

Evidence Examples

- Faculty hiring rubrics and evaluation criteria
- Teaching demonstration assessment forms
- Faculty workload and sufficiency analyses
- Faculty credential and experience summaries

II. Educational Quality and Student Learning

(HLC Criterion 4 | MSCHE Standard V | SACSCOC Standard 8 | NECHE Standard 4 | WSCUC CFR 2.3)

Narrative Alignment

Cybersecurity educator recruitment and retention directly support educational quality and student learning outcomes. Faculty are selected based on their ability to translate complex cybersecurity concepts into effective instructional practice aligned with program objectives.

Instructional quality is reinforced through onboarding, mentoring, and discipline-specific professional development.

Faculty stability supports curriculum coherence, consistent assessment practices, and continuous improvement in student learning outcomes.

Faculty evaluation processes focus on instructional effectiveness, student engagement, and alignment with learning outcomes, reinforcing a culture of teaching excellence.

Evidence Examples

- Curriculum maps linking faculty expertise to course outcomes
- Student learning assessment reports
- Course evaluation summaries and instructional feedback
- Professional development participation records

III. Institutional Effectiveness and Continuous Improvement

(HLC Criterion 4 | MSCHE Standard VI | SACSCOC Standard 7 | NECHE Standard 2 | WSCUC CFR 4)

Narrative Alignment

The institution integrates cybersecurity educator recruitment and retention into its institutional effectiveness framework. Recruitment outcomes, early retention, instructional performance, and faculty satisfaction are tracked and reviewed regularly.

Feedback from faculty and students informs continuous improvement of hiring practices, onboarding processes, and professional development offerings. Recruitment and retention practices are revised based on evidence rather than assumption.

This systematic approach ensures that faculty workforce development contributes measurably to institutional effectiveness and student success.

Evidence Examples

- Recruitment and retention metrics dashboards
- Faculty satisfaction and feedback surveys
- Continuous improvement action plans
- Assessment cycle documentation

IV. Governance, Leadership, and Administrative Capacity

(HLC Criterion 2 | MSCHE Standard VII | SACSCOC Standard 5 | NECHE Standard 3 | WSCUC CFR 3)

Narrative Alignment

Leadership oversight ensures cybersecurity educator recruitment and retention align with institutional mission and strategic priorities. Clear governance structures define roles and decision authority for faculty hiring, evaluation, and professional development.

Executive leadership remains accountable for recruitment outcomes, faculty sufficiency, and retention. Recruitment practices are documented to preserve institutional memory and ensure continuity across leadership transitions.

Administrative capacity supports effective implementation of recruitment and retention systems, demonstrating institutional readiness and stability.

Evidence Examples

- Governance and committee charters
- Leadership role descriptions

- Recruitment process documentation
- Succession planning materials

V. Strategic Planning and Sustainability

(HLC Criterion 5 | MSCHE Standard II | SACSCOC Standard 9 | NECHE Standard 1 | WSCUC CFR 1)

Narrative Alignment

Cybersecurity educator workforce planning is embedded within institutional strategic planning. Anticipated enrollment trends, program growth, and curriculum evolution inform proactive recruitment strategies.

The institution plans for faculty succession, professional development, and retention to ensure long-term instructional capacity. Recruitment and retention investments are aligned with budget planning and program sustainability goals.

This forward-looking approach supports institutional resilience and long-term educational quality.

Evidence Examples

- Strategic plan excerpts referencing faculty workforce planning
- Enrollment and staffing projections
- Budget alignment documentation
- Long-term program development plans

Regional Accreditation Insert-Ready Summary Statement

The institution employs a systematic, evidence-based approach to cybersecurity educator recruitment and retention that supports faculty sufficiency, instructional quality, institutional effectiveness, and long-term sustainability.

Faculty are selected and supported based on demonstrated instructional capability, professional credibility, and alignment with program learning outcomes. Recruitment, onboarding, evaluation, and professional development are integrated into institutional effectiveness and strategic planning processes, ensuring continuity, compliance with regional accreditation expectations, and sustained student success.

Self-Study Chapter Framework Appendix

Cybersecurity Educator Recruitment, Retention, and Institutional Effectiveness

X.1 Purpose and Context

This chapter documents how the institution ensures the recruitment, development, and retention of qualified cybersecurity educators in alignment with institutional mission, educational quality, and long-term sustainability. Given the applied and rapidly evolving nature of cybersecurity as a discipline, the institution approaches faculty workforce development as a strategic and continuous institutional function, rather than a transactional hiring activity.

Cybersecurity programs rely on instructional continuity, professional relevance, and faculty credibility to support student learning outcomes and workforce readiness. Persistent national shortages of cybersecurity educators heighten institutional responsibility to design recruitment and retention systems intentionally. This chapter demonstrates how the institution addresses that responsibility through structured hiring frameworks, onboarding and professional development, governance oversight, and continuous improvement mechanisms.

The practices described align with regional accreditation expectations related to faculty qualifications and sufficiency, educational quality, institutional effectiveness, governance, and strategic planning.

X.2 Faculty Qualifications and Sufficiency

The institution ensures cybersecurity educators are qualified for their assigned instructional responsibilities through a holistic evaluation of academic preparation, professional experience, and demonstrated instructional capability.

Faculty hiring emphasizes alignment with course and program learning outcomes rather than reliance on credentials alone.

Hiring decisions are guided by structured evaluation frameworks that assess four core dimensions: instructional capability, instructional readiness, professional credibility, and motivation for teaching. Candidates demonstrate instructional effectiveness through scenario-based interviews and teaching demonstrations aligned with actual curriculum requirements. This approach ensures faculty possess both disciplinary expertise and the ability to translate that expertise into effective instruction.

Faculty sufficiency is monitored through enrollment projections, workload analysis, and early retention tracking to ensure instructional continuity. When gaps are identified, recruitment strategies are adjusted proactively rather than reactively.

Representative Evidence

- Faculty hiring rubrics and evaluation criteria
- Teaching demonstration assessment forms
- Faculty credential and professional experience summaries
- Faculty workload and sufficiency analyses

X.3 Educational Quality and Student Learning

Cybersecurity educator recruitment and retention are directly linked to educational quality and student learning outcomes. Faculty are selected based on their ability to deliver applied, current, and coherent instruction aligned with program objectives and workforce expectations.

Instructional quality is reinforced through onboarding, mentoring, and discipline-specific professional development that supports effective teaching practice. Faculty stability contributes to curriculum coherence, consistent assessment practices, and meaningful student engagement across courses and modalities.

Faculty evaluation processes emphasize instructional effectiveness, alignment with learning outcomes, and continuous improvement rather than procedural compliance alone. Student learning data and course evaluations inform faculty development and instructional refinement.

Representative Evidence

- Curriculum maps linking faculty expertise to learning outcomes
- Student learning assessment reports
- Course evaluation summaries
- Faculty professional development records

X.4 Institutional Effectiveness and Continuous Improvement

The institution integrates cybersecurity educator recruitment and retention into its broader institutional effectiveness framework. Recruitment outcomes, early faculty retention, instructional performance, and faculty satisfaction are tracked and reviewed regularly as part of continuous improvement processes.

Feedback from faculty and students informs refinement of hiring practices, onboarding structures, and professional development offerings. Recruitment practices are evaluated based on evidence rather than assumption, ensuring responsiveness to program needs and institutional goals.

This systematic approach ensures faculty workforce development contributes measurably to student success, program stability, and institutional effectiveness.

Representative Evidence

- Recruitment and retention metrics dashboards
- Faculty satisfaction and feedback surveys
- Continuous improvement action plans
- Assessment cycle documentation

X.5 Governance, Leadership, and Administrative Capacity

Leadership oversight ensures cybersecurity educator recruitment and retention align with institutional mission and strategic priorities. Governance structures clearly define roles and decision authority for faculty hiring, evaluation, onboarding, and professional development.

Executive leadership remains accountable for faculty sufficiency, recruitment outcomes, and retention. Recruitment processes are documented to preserve institutional memory and ensure continuity across leadership transitions. Coordination between academic leadership and human resources supports consistency and compliance.

Administrative capacity supports effective implementation of recruitment and retention systems, demonstrating institutional readiness and organizational stability.

Representative Evidence

- Governance and committee charters
- Leadership role descriptions
- Recruitment process documentation

- Succession planning materials

X.6 Strategic Planning and Sustainability

Cybersecurity educator workforce planning is embedded within institutional strategic planning processes. Anticipated enrollment trends, program growth, curriculum evolution, and faculty succession inform proactive recruitment strategies.

The institution plans for long-term faculty capacity through targeted recruitment, onboarding investment, professional development, and retention initiatives. Budget planning aligns with workforce sustainability goals to support instructional continuity and program quality.

This forward-looking approach reduces reliance on crisis hiring and supports long-term institutional resilience.

Representative Evidence

- Strategic plan excerpts referencing faculty workforce planning
- Enrollment and staffing projections
- Budget alignment documentation
- Long-term program development plans

X.7 Summary and Assurance of Compliance

The institution employs a systematic, evidence-based approach to cybersecurity educator recruitment and retention that supports faculty qualifications and sufficiency, educational quality, institutional effectiveness, governance integrity, and strategic sustainability. Faculty are selected and supported based on demonstrated instructional capability, professional credibility, and alignment with program learning outcomes.

Recruitment, onboarding, evaluation, and professional development are integrated into continuous improvement and strategic planning processes. Leadership oversight and governance clarity ensure accountability and continuity. Through these practices, the institution demonstrates compliance with regional accreditation expectations and a sustained commitment to student success and workforce readiness.

Insert-Ready Assurance Statement (Optional)

The institution's approach to cybersecurity educator recruitment and retention reflects intentional design, leadership stewardship, and continuous improvement. Faculty workforce development is treated as a strategic institutional function that supports instructional quality, student learning outcomes, and long-term program sustainability, consistent with regional accreditation standards.

Mock Regional Reviewer Questions

With Model Institutional Responses

(Cybersecurity Educator Recruitment, Retention, and Institutional Effectiveness)

These questions reflect the **actual lines of inquiry** reviewers use during self-study review, off-site analysis, and on-site interviews.

Question 1

How does the institution ensure cybersecurity faculty are appropriately qualified for their instructional responsibilities?

Model Response

The institution evaluates cybersecurity faculty qualifications holistically, considering academic preparation, relevant professional experience, and demonstrated instructional capability. Given the applied nature of cybersecurity, faculty selection emphasizes alignment between professional expertise and course learning outcomes rather than reliance on credentials alone.

Faculty candidates demonstrate instructional effectiveness through structured interviews and teaching demonstrations aligned to curriculum requirements. This approach ensures faculty possess both disciplinary expertise and the ability to translate that expertise into effective teaching practice. Faculty qualifications are reviewed regularly to ensure continued alignment with program needs.

Question 2

How does the institution ensure faculty sufficiency and instructional continuity within cybersecurity programs?

Model Response

Faculty sufficiency is monitored through enrollment trends, workload analysis, and early retention tracking. The institution engages in proactive workforce planning to anticipate instructional needs related to program growth, curriculum evolution, and faculty transitions.

Recruitment is treated as a continuous process rather than a reactive response to vacancies. Onboarding and mentoring structures support early integration and reduce attrition risk, ensuring instructional continuity and program stability.

Question 3

How do faculty recruitment and retention practices support educational quality and student learning outcomes?

Model Response

Faculty recruitment and retention are intentionally aligned with educational quality objectives. Cybersecurity educators are selected based on their ability to deliver applied, current instruction aligned with program learning outcomes and workforce expectations.

Retention practices such as mentorship, professional development, and workload calibration support instructional consistency. Faculty evaluation processes emphasize instructional effectiveness and student engagement, ensuring teaching quality contributes directly to student learning outcomes.

Question 4

How does the institution evaluate the effectiveness of its cybersecurity faculty recruitment and retention practices?

Model Response

The institution evaluates recruitment and retention effectiveness using both quantitative and qualitative measures. These include time to productivity, early faculty retention, instructional performance indicators, and faculty satisfaction feedback.

Results are reviewed through institutional effectiveness processes and used to refine hiring frameworks, onboarding structures, and professional development offerings. This evidence-based approach ensures continuous improvement rather than static compliance.

Question 5

How does governance support consistent and effective faculty hiring practices?

Model Response

Clear governance structures define roles and decision authority for faculty hiring, evaluation, and professional development. Academic leadership, human resources, and search committees operate within shared frameworks to ensure consistency and alignment.

Leadership oversight ensures accountability for recruitment outcomes, while documentation preserves institutional memory across leadership transitions. This structure supports stability, fairness, and compliance.

Question 6

How does the institution ensure recruitment practices remain effective during leadership transitions?

Model Response

Recruitment processes are documented and institutionalized rather than dependent on individual leaders. Search committee training, standardized evaluation tools, and governance clarity preserve continuity.

Incoming leaders receive orientation to recruitment frameworks and workforce planning processes. This approach ensures recruitment capability remains stable across leadership changes.

Question 7

How does cybersecurity faculty workforce planning align with institutional strategic planning?

Model Response

Cybersecurity faculty workforce planning is embedded within institutional strategic planning processes. Enrollment projections, program development goals, and anticipated faculty transitions inform proactive recruitment strategies.

Budget planning aligns with workforce sustainability objectives to support instructional continuity and long-term program quality. This integration ensures recruitment supports institutional mission and strategic priorities.

Question 8

What evidence demonstrates the institution's commitment to continuous improvement in faculty recruitment and retention?

Model Response

The institution maintains structured feedback mechanisms, including faculty surveys, early retention reviews, and student feedback analysis. These data inform periodic review and refinement of recruitment, onboarding, and professional development practices.

Documented action plans demonstrate responsiveness to identified gaps. Leadership oversight ensures follow-through and accountability, reinforcing a culture of continuous improvement.

Integration Into a Full Institutional Self-Study Outline

(Regional Accreditation Ready)

Below is a **full self-study outline** showing **exact placement** of the chapter you developed, ensuring coherence and reviewer flow.

Institutional Self-Study Outline

(Regional Accreditation)

Chapter 1

Mission, Integrity, and Institutional Purpose

- Mission alignment
- Ethical conduct
- Public responsibility

Chapter 2

Governance, Leadership, and Administrative Capacity

- Board oversight
- Executive leadership roles
- Decision authority and accountability
- Succession planning

Chapter 3

Strategic Planning and Institutional Sustainability

- Strategic planning processes
- Resource alignment

- Workforce planning integration
- Long-term program viability

Chapter 4

Academic Programs and Curriculum Quality

- Program design and coherence
- Curriculum review processes
- Alignment with workforce needs

Chapter 5

Faculty Qualifications, Sufficiency, and Development

- Cybersecurity educator recruitment and retention *(Primary anchor)*
- Faculty hiring frameworks
- Onboarding and mentoring
- Professional development
- Evaluation and recognition

This is where your integrated chapter sits as Chapter 5 or a major subsection

Chapter 6

Teaching Effectiveness and Student Learning

- Instructional quality assurance
- Faculty evaluation processes
- Assessment of student learning outcomes

- Continuous improvement

Chapter 7

Institutional Effectiveness

- Data-informed decision making
- Continuous improvement cycles
- Recruitment and retention metrics
- Evidence of impact

Chapter 8

Student Support and Learning Resources

- Academic support services
- Technology and lab resources
- Faculty support infrastructure

Chapter 9

Accreditation Compliance Summary and Assurance

- Crosswalk of standards to evidence
- Summary of compliance
- Institutional assurance statements

Appendices

- DEAC-Aligned Recruitment Appendix
- Regional Accreditation Recruitment Appendix
- HR Toolkits and Hiring Frameworks

- Search Committee Training Materials
- Faculty Evaluation Rubrics

Why This Works for Reviewers

- Your cybersecurity faculty practices are not isolated
- They are embedded in faculty, academic quality, effectiveness, and strategy
- Evidence is distributed where reviewers expect to see it
- The narrative avoids defensiveness and emphasizes systems

www.ingramcontent.com/pod-product-compliance
Lightning Source LLC
LaVergne TN
LVHW091004080826
845145LV00003B/1121

* 9 7 8 1 9 7 2 1 5 4 0 1 4 *